CARLENE FIRMIN,
MICHELLE LEFEVRE,
NATHALIE HUEGLER
AND DELPHINE PEACE

T0277340

SAFEGUARDING YOUNG PEOPLE BEYOND THE FAMILY HOME

Responding to Extra-Familial Risks and Harms

First published in Great Britain in 2022 by

Policy Press, an imprint of
Bristol University Press
University of Bristol
1–9 Old Park Hill
Bristol
BS2 8BB
UK
t: +44 (0)117 374 6645
e: bup-info@bristol.ac.uk

Details of international sales and distribution partners are available at
policy.bristoluniversitypress.co.uk

British Library Cataloguing in Publication Data
A catalogue record for this book is available from the British Library

ISBN 978-1-4473-6725-3 paperback
ISBN 978-1-4473-6726-0 ePub
ISBN 978-1-4473-6727-7 OA Pdf

Contents

List of figures and tables

Figures

Tables

Acknowledgements

This book would not have happened without the support of the Economic and Social Research Council. Its four years funding for the Innovate Project enabled us to conduct the evidence review upon which this book is based and gave us the time to write it. We are grateful for the ideas shared by, and the many discussions with, all members of the Innovate Project. In particular, we thank Katie Latimer, now moved on, who contributed to the original evidence review, and Kristi Hickle and Gillian Ruch, who read draft chapters. We owe a particular debt of gratitude to Lauren Wroe, from Durham University, who provided a thorough critical and textual review of the whole text. We wish to acknowledge the additional financial support from the University of Sussex and Durham University, which has enabled the electronic version of this book to be published open access. We hope that this means it will be shared widely in the practice field to facilitate the further development of services. Finally, we acknowledge the important contribution to this book of all the young people, parents, carers and practitioners who, in the studies we reviewed, shared their perspectives on service approaches to preventing and addressing extra-familial risks and harms.

ONE

The emerging concept of extra-familial risks and harms

Introduction

> Someone walked into the school, where I was supposed
> to feel safe, took me away from the people who were
> supposed to protect me and stripped me naked, while
> on my period. ... On the top of preparing for the most
> important exams of my life. I can't go a single day without
> wanting to scream, shout, cry or just give up. ... I feel
> like I'm locked in a box, and no one can see or cares
> that I just want to go back to feeling safe again, my box
> is collapsing around me, and no-one wants to help. ...
> I don't know if I'm going to feel normal again. I don't
> know how long it will take to repair my box. But I do
> know this can't happen to anyone, ever again. (Child Q,
> quoted in Gamble and McCallum, 2022: 11)

In the final stages of writing this book, the voice of Child Q
was heard by the UK public. Child Q, a 15-year-old Black
young woman from London, experienced significant harm in
a place – as she described – where she was supposed to be safe.
The people who harmed her were not her parents or carers;

they were school staff, who pulled her out of an exam and called the police because they thought she smelled of cannabis and might be carrying drugs, and they were police officers, who strip-searched her and examined her intimate body parts in the school medical room, without an appropriate adult present and while she was menstruating. This professional response appeared to be driven by public safety and criminal justice concerns, with no regard for the welfare implications of Child Q's possible involvement in offending. There appeared to be no consideration of Child Q's rights to privacy, nor of the harm that might be caused to her by the professional response – a response that was later constructed as a safeguarding issue by a local child safeguarding practice review instituted to consider this situation (Gamble and McCallum, 2022).

The voice of Child Q brings into focus an issue that UK practitioners, policymakers and families have been grappling with over recent decades: how should professionals, and the systems within which they work, respond to young people who are caught up in criminal, dangerous or harmful contexts and situations involving peers and adults unconnected to young people's families or homes? The risks and harms that have provoked increasing public attention over the past decade or so have included criminal and sexual exploitation, weapon-enabled violence, sexual harassment and abuse in schools, and abuse in young people's romantic or intimate relationships (Coy, 2017; Lloyd, 2019; Robinson et al, 2019; National Youth Agency, 2020). For the most part, public attention has been on the nature of such harms themselves, but the extent to which governments and statutory services have failed to address risks and their impacts, and indeed may have even exacerbated, facilitated or created the conditions for these harms to occur, continues to generate substantial concern (Ofsted, 2019; Child Safeguarding Practice Review Panel, 2020; McAlister, 2021; Independent Anti-Slavery Commissioner, 2022).

These 'extra-familial risks and harms' (EFRH) are not, by definition, caused by parental abuse, neglect or inadequate parenting, but they still pose a risk of significant harm to young people's welfare. As a result, they are increasingly being framed, in the UK at least, as safeguarding issues, and social workers are centre stage in developing and coordinating safety plans and protection-oriented interventions (Department of Health, 2017; Her Majesty's Government, 2018; Scottish Government, 2021; Welsh Government, 2021). Yet, social work roles, and the safeguarding systems in which they are deployed, were not designed with these EFRH in mind; this presents complex challenges for service and policy design. Additional funding has been made available, particularly in England (Department for Education, 2021), to support voluntary and statutory services in innovating more effective responses to these contemporary issues, with a view to safeguarding young people, promoting their welfare and attending to public protection considerations. However, the evidence base for many of these innovations is in its infancy (FitzSimons and McCracken, 2020), and questions remain about the feasibility of offering safeguarding and wider social work responses to risks beyond families. This is further complicated when considering that 'youth' and adolescence are increasingly defined as ranging from the early teens to the mid-20s (Sawyer et al, 2018), meaning that in many countries, gaps are likely to exist between child welfare and adult support systems (Holmes and Smale, 2018). Indeed, in this book, we go on to consider system and practice responses to EFRH involving young people from the age of 12 through to 25, as this more inclusive definition reflects how the dynamics of adolescent development and vulnerability to EFRH often continue beyond the age of 18 (Hanson and Holmes, 2014).

The authors of this book have come together since 2019 with other colleagues from the Universities of Sussex, Durham and Bedfordshire in the UK, the charity Research in Practice, and the social enterprise Innovation Unit to examine and contribute answers to these questions. Our Innovate Project (see: www. theinnovateproject.co.uk), funded by the Economic and Social Research Council in the UK, is studying what happens as new practice systems and interventions for young people exposed to EFRH are developed, and seeks to establish what approaches might be effective. In 2020, we undertook a rapid evidence review of what was already known about social care responses, and their effectiveness in dealing with EFRH, to inform the early stages of the Innovate Project. In this book, we present the results of this exercise and use them to build a framework for developing policy and service responses to EFRH in the future. While our recommendations principally target a UK service landscape, the evidence utilised spans multiple countries, mainly in the Global North, where formal child welfare systems centring social work respond to young people experiencing EFRH (and where the lack of similar systems for older young people often leads to gaps in transitions to adulthood). As such, the implications of our work may be of relevance to a range of international contexts that are also grappling with how best to safeguard young people harmed beyond their homes.

EFRH: what is included?

Policy in the four countries of the UK increasingly includes reference to such phrases as 'extra-familial risk and harms' (Scottish Government, 2021), 'extra-familial threats' (Her Majesty's Government, 2018), 'extra-familial abuse' (Welsh Government, 2021), 'risk(s) or harms outside the (family) home or setting' (Department of Health, 2017; Her Majesty's Government, 2018; Stanley, 2020; McAlister, 2021) and 'risks and harm young people face beyond the family home' (Scottish Government, 2021). Our inclusive category descriptor of 'extra-familial risks and harms' serves two purposes. First, it is intended to distinguish *risks* beyond the home as being part of the terrain that most, if not all, young people encounter in adolescence, whereas only for some will risky relationships and situations escalate to incur *harm*. Second, pluralising the terms is intended to reflect the range and diversity of risk and harm types.

The EFRH elaborated by these policy documents and practice guidance include:

- sexual exploitation of children and young people by adults;
- criminal exploitation of children and young people, particularly for the purposes of cultivating, trafficking, distributing and/or selling illegal substances;
- serious physical violence between young people, including weapon-enabled violence, some of which may be connected to organised criminal groups;
- peer-to-peer sexual abuse and other forms of harmful (problematic or inappropriate) sexual behaviour displayed by young people towards their peers;
- the radicalisation of young people into political or religious ideologies that place them at risk of physical or emotional harm; and
- physical, sexual or emotional abuse, and/or coercive control, young people may experience in their own romantic/intimate relationships.

In England and Scotland, and to a lesser extent in Wales and Northern Ireland, framing harm in this manner foregrounds extra-familial dynamics in two ways: first, in respect of the relationship(s) in which the harm occurs (interpersonal but not familial); and, second, in recognition of the social/physical contexts beyond family homes where much of this harm takes place (in such settings as schools, neighbourhood locations, organised criminal networks and online social media platforms, for example). We acknowledge that such a grouping is a construct; there are a range of other ways in which these harms may be clustered or disaggregated. Additionally, risks and harms may, of course, be experienced away from where the young person is living but still involve family members, and they may happen inside the young person's abode but not in conjunction with a family member. However, this approach to grouping these different forms of EFRH is supported not only by policy, but also by researchers and practitioners who have increasingly highlighted how the extra-familial dynamics of these harms warrant specific attention if effective responses are to be offered (Hanson and Holmes, 2014; Brandon et al, 2020; Wroe and Lloyd, 2020).

The category of EFRH communicates something of significance in relation to the *shortfalls* of safeguarding and welfare systems in countries like the UK, rather than just characterising the risks and harms themselves. Importantly, the child protection elements of safeguarding systems in the UK, and other Global North countries that we go on to discuss in this book, were not designed to deal with risks beyond the home and family, though they are leveraged when young people (under 18) are at risk of significant harm. It is this, in our view, that renders the creation of the EFRH category necessary.

Child and family social work in the UK, and in a range of other countries in the Global North, operates within legislative and practice frameworks predicated on the idea that if a child is at risk of harm, this will be attributable to action or inaction by their parents or carers (Fong and Cardoso, 2010; Radford et al, 2017; Firmin, 2020). As a consequence, the majority of interventions are directed towards the parenting role and its perceived inadequacies. While neglect and familial abuse may increase the vulnerability of a young person to experiencing risks or harm, young people may also become involved in EFRH when parents are taking all necessary steps to keep their children safe (Pike et al, 2019; Child Safeguarding Practice Review Panel, 2020). Moreover, even in instances where young people affected by EFRH are living in families where there are additional challenges and needs, it is rare that intervention with parents alone will address the source of the harm in question. As such, assessment of parental capacity to protect and solely parent-focused interventions are likely to prove insufficient in social work responses to EFRH.

It is perhaps not surprising that these shortfalls become even more evident for older adolescents once they reach the age of 18. In the UK, adult safeguarding services tend to respond only in cases where a young person is considered to have exclusively defined needs for 'care and support', as set out in the Care Act 2014, a criterion that many young people experiencing EFRH do not meet. Holmes (2022: 8–9) describes a self-enforcing paradoxical situation for young people both under and over 18 where safeguarding:

> acts not as a verb – something to do with a person when their safety is undermined, but as a noun – a threshold to be reached, a place that many people cannot access despite their safety being undermined. ... So it is 'not safeguarding' if the person does not receive a safeguarding response, and they do not receive a response if their situation is understood in procedural terms to be 'not safeguarding'. This self-reinforcing loop, with terms defining actions that in turn prescribe the terms, undermines the sector's ability to adapt and refine its response to emerging need and evidence. (Holmes, 2022: 8–9)

Hence, gaps in addressing EFRH are both created and perpetuated by the very systems that should provide protection and support. Our review indicates that the mechanisms of these shortfalls are embedded in system- and service-specific procedures; however, the phenomenon of excluding EFRH from safeguarding domains is widespread across countries in the Global North.

Despite the merits of an overarching EFRH category, it is important to note from the outset that there are limitations to this approach – limitations that we will revisit at various points in the book. One of most note is the variable evidence base for social care responses to each type of harm included in this umbrella category. Evidence regarding effectiveness is more established for practice systems and models that address child sexual exploitation (CSE), for example, compared with responses to radicalisation or serious youth violence, which remain heavily rooted in policing and crime prevention practices (Chisolm and Coulter, 2017; Association of Directors of Children's Services, 2019). Moreover, the manifestations of some types of harm, the terms used to demarcate them and the delineation of appropriate or necessary social care responses can vary over geographical boundaries. While there is increasing consensus across the Global North as to what is encompassed by such terms as 'child sexual exploitation' and 'domestic minor sex trafficking', the concept of child *criminal* exploitation is less established outside of the UK, and its manifestations are more differentiated – for example, the particular form of child trafficking by organised crime groups to achieve the distribution of drugs from urban to rural counties ('County Lines') appears quite specific to the UK, possibly related to the country's smaller size and accessible transport links (Coomer and Moyle, 2017). It must also be acknowledged that there are a range of other harms unrelated to home or family that can affect young people, such as poverty, inequality of opportunity and institutional racism or other forms of institutional harm. These are not the focus of this book per se, even though they may contribute to or compound EFRH (Featherstone et al, 2018). Indeed, the case of Child Q highlights the complex intersections of institutional harm and EFRH, whereby, paradoxically, responses that should address harm become themselves abusive.

The emergent policy and practice focus in the UK on safeguarding harms beyond the home and family, alongside the shared system challenges that come with offering a child protection, and wider safeguarding, response to this group of harms, warrant the contribution that this book offers. We reflect on these challenges throughout this book and offer subcategories of EFRH as harm-type clusters to explore what some of these variations and associated limitations imply for social care responses.

From youth justice to welfare: the emergent policy response in the UK

In the 1990s and 2000s, issues associated with EFRH in the UK were predominantly viewed through the prisms of 'anti-social behaviour', youth crime and individualising discourses of social exclusion (Her Majesty's Government, 2005; Rogowski, 2010). This involved, to a large degree, an emphasis on responsibility and blame being placed on young people for what were considered dangerous, disruptive or otherwise concerning behaviours (such as the use of drugs, sexual activity construed as 'promiscuity', excessive alcohol consumption and teenage pregnancy, as well as a 'failure' to participate in education, training or work). While highly publicised cases of child maltreatment repeatedly drew attention to the failures of statutory systems to protect young children from harm inflicted by family members (and, at times, triggered legislative reforms), the language of safeguarding in relation to risks and harm during adolescence was notably absent (Her Majesty's Government, 2005; Department for Education and Skills, 2007).

This framing occurred against the backdrop of the Children Act 1989, introduced in England and Wales, which underpins England's safeguarding system to the present day. A co-author of this legislation, Baroness Hale, described one of the intentions behind the act's design as being to separate out legal proceedings against parents (the child protection system) from those against young people themselves (the youth justice system); the latter was designated for 'delinquent or naughty children – those who were out of control, falling into bad associations or in moral danger – with the former intended for children who were suffering or at risk of suffering neglect or abuse' (Lady Hale, 2019: 2). It should be noted that youth offending legislation, introduced during a similar time period in England and Wales, sought to shift youth justice services from punitive responses towards a more welfare- or treatment-focused approach (Rogowski, 2010). In contrast to the separate systems in England and Wales, the Scottish Children's Hearing System, introduced in 1971, provided a joined-up child welfare response to children under 16 in conflict with the law and those in need of care and protection; however, young people aged 16 to 17 remained in the remit of adult courts (Children and Young People's Centre for Justice, 2021).

In the early 2010s, numerous inquiries into CSE drew attention to shortfalls in professional responses to this form of EFRH (Berelowitz et al, 2012, 2015; Coffey, 2014; Jay, 2014; Bedford, 2015). In particular, they evidenced how safeguarding services framed sexually exploited young people as responsible and agentic, and therefore potentially complicit in their own abuse:

> Children and young people who were being sexually exploited were frequently described by professionals in many localities as being 'promiscuous', 'liking the glamour', engaging in 'risky behaviour' and being generally badly behaved. Some of the most common phrases used to describe the young person's behaviour were: 'prostituting herself', 'sexually available' and 'asking for it'. (Berelowitz et al, 2012: 12)

While these inquiries led to an increased recognition of the safeguarding needs of some sexually exploited young people, concerns around the under-identification of victimisation persisted, particularly regarding young people with disabilities and those who were racially minoritised (Berelowitz et al, 2015).

A further development impacting safeguarding practice at the time came in the form of a landmark court decision in 2009 (*R [G] v Southwark* [2009] UKHL 26), concerning the duties of social care departments to homeless young people aged 16 and 17, who had hitherto often been considered only through the prism of their housing needs. This judgment concluded that when a 16- or 17-year-old presents as homeless, the local authority children's services should undertake the initial assessment, not the housing department. This milestone drew further attention to young people 'at the edge of [out-of-home] care' (Boddy et al, 2009: 2), including those whose families were struggling to care for them due to EFRH.

The aforementioned policy concerns about the high rates of adolescents in out-of-home care and failures to protect young people from sexual exploitation came to the fore at a time of increasing debate in the UK about how best to safeguard young people. The needs, preferences and degree of autonomy of young people in adolescence may differ substantially from those of younger children, and these differences are not always managed well by safeguarding systems (Ofsted, 2011; Hanson and Holmes, 2014). Nearly a third of serious case reviews conducted in England between 2014 and 2017 focused on the serious or fatal maltreatment of young people aged 11 and over where there had been cause for concern about the safeguarding response (Brandon et al, 2020). Macro-analysis of these reviews revealed that, 'For many of these young people, their age and behaviour led to professionals viewing them more as adults rather than vulnerable young people with little possibility of changing their behaviour and circumstances' (Sidebotham et al, 2016: 127).

In 2014, the Association of Directors of Children's Services in England commissioned a report by the national charity Research in Practice on the evidence around adolescence and risk. The report critiqued England's child protection system for its failure to enable effective, age-appropriate, strengths-based approaches involving young people, families, peers and communities in relation to EFRH (Hanson and Holmes, 2014). The authors proposed a shift towards approaches that reduce exposure to risks during adolescence, build resilience by working with young people as partners and harness the strengths and opportunities of adolescence, while avoiding blaming and labelling approaches.

Research, inspection reports, public inquiries, case reviews and government reports from 2015 onwards in the UK have continued to express concern about the adequacy of systems to safeguard young people as child criminal exploitation, peer-to-peer sexual abuse in schools and radicalisation started to be recognised as forms of EFRH (Child Safeguarding Practice Review Panel, 2020; Kirkman, 2020; Department for Education, 2021; Estyn, 2021; Ofsted, 2021). Safeguarding policies and guidance have been adapted in response to these rapidly changing policy, practice and research landscapes to constitute young people's involvement in exploitation, abuse and violence in contexts beyond the family home as a safeguarding concern (rather than solely a matter of youth crime or anti-social behaviour) and to mandate social care responses where young people under 18 are concerned.

In light of this shifting policy concern, government departments and national funders in the UK have resourced a range of interventions designed to better meet the needs of young people, including those at risk of harm beyond their family homes and relationships. Innovations have included: the Achieving Change Together framework, used by interdisciplinary 'complex safeguarding' teams in Greater Manchester to promote collaborative approaches to assessment and planning with young people affected by CSE (Scott et al, 2017a); the No Wrong Door initiative, offering integrated support to young people aged 12 to 25 at risk of entering the care system (Lushey et al, 2017); and the Disrupting Exploitation programme, run by voluntary organisation The Children's Society to intervene with situations and systems, as well as individuals, impacted by exploitation (Cordis Bright, 2019).

Simultaneously, concepts have been introduced into national policy and research contexts to assist the aforementioned efforts at service redesign. Contextual Safeguarding – an approach developed by the first author and colleagues (Firmin et al, 2016) – highlighted the significance of peer and community contexts in cases of EFRH, and how this contrasted with the individualised, family-focused character of interventions within the English child protection system. As a result, Contextual Safeguarding promoted the assessment of, and intervention with, a range of contexts beyond families (as well as associated relationships and spaces) within which EFRH occurs, while also recognising and utilising their inherent strengths and resources. Other developments included an increasing recognition of the relevance of trauma-informed approaches across England, Wales and Scotland (Wilkinson, 2018; Scottish Government, 2021; Welsh Government, 2021) and, as part of this, the need to address the trauma that EFRH may induce. In 2018, the formulation of transitional safeguarding as a concept highlighted the need for support and safeguarding systems to take account of young people's continuing needs into adulthood (Holmes and Smale, 2018).

The aforementioned policy and practice developments indicate attempts to reconcile the split referred to earlier in this chapter between welfare (particularly child protection) and justice responses to young people – a split instigated by the introduction of the Children Act 1989. They denote a recognition of how the separation of service responses to young people harmed by their parents or carers from those to young people who harm themselves or others has been unable to accommodate the needs of young people affected by EFRH, or indeed of young people during the period of adolescence more broadly. However, the development of more welfare-oriented responses to young people affected by EFRH has been fraught with challenges, both in their formulation and in their implementation. While the policy trajectory outlined thus far is unique to the UK, the associated challenges are not. We now outline some shared obstacles in system responses to forms of EFRH in different parts of the Global North, before setting out how this book seeks to support efforts to resolve some of them.

Adopting a welfare-based approach to EFRH: shared global challenges but divergent responses

Despite this increased recognition of the nature of EFRH and its safeguarding implications in UK *policy*, concerns remain about the adequacy of social care responses *in practice*. In particular, there are concerns about the ability of social care systems in the UK to adopt a welfare (and, where required, child protection) approach to harms that were not in mind at the point of system design (McAlister, 2021). These concerns are not limited to the UK. Struggles to develop welfare and safeguarding systems capable of engaging with the specific complexities of supporting young people affected by EFRH are recognisable in research from various countries in the Global North (Radford et al, 2015; Organization for Security and Co-operation in Europe, 2019; Gregulska et al, 2020), most notably, in the study of CSE and trafficking. This literature identifies, in particular, the struggle of practitioners and systems to work with the agentic nature of young people who have been exploited (particularly those who go missing from home), to develop a welfare rather than justice-oriented response and, as part of this, to respond to young people who straddle victim–perpetrator identities. These struggles occur in wider contexts of child protection pathways designed to target families and wider interventions that disrupt the actions of individual young people and not the harmful situations in which they act.

Balancing rights to protection and autonomy

One key challenge that EFRH poses to organisations, multi-agency networks and individual practitioners relates to a foundational dilemma across all branches of welfare services: how to balance paradigms of care and control when individuals are at risk and/or pose risk to others (Payne, 2020). Statutory agencies across a range of countries have often failed to recognise EFRH as a form of abuse, castigating, ignoring or criminalising children, rather than protecting them. When the failure to address CSE came to light in the UK, for example, through whistleblowing, investigative reporting and public inquiries (Berelowitz et al, 2012 2015; Coffey, 2014; Jay, 2014), the public outcry and government response led to a decisive swing towards a protective stance. Many young people caught up in sexual exploitation were less likely to be seen as blameworthy autonomous agents who were 'putting themselves at risk' to be reconstructed as vulnerable child victims (Lefevre et al, 2019: 1840). Multi-agency safeguarding networks and processes were put in place to assess and address risks, and in some cases, high levels of support were offered to young people and their families, including through a range of partnerships with the voluntary and community sectors. However, this recognition of vulnerability and victimhood has not necessarily been true for working-class girls (Brown, 2019), boys and young men (McNaughton Nicholls et al, 2014), Black young people (Davis, 2019; Davis and Marsh, 2020), and young South Asian women (Gutierrez and Chawla, 2017).

Meanwhile, professional systems across a range of countries have continued to struggle with balancing and reconciling young people's right to safety and protection with their right to voice, privacy and autonomy, as well as with the public's right to protection (Sapiro et al, 2016). For some young people, this has meant unwelcomingly high levels of intrusion into their personal and social lives, as the threshold for professional suspicion in relation to their behaviour is very low (Wroe and Lloyd, 2020). Young people at risk of exploitation have described their mobile phones and other property being searched or confiscated, their peer relationships being scrutinised and controlled, and their underwear being taken away for forensic examination of sexual activity in the guise of 'protection at all costs' (Lefevre et al, 2019: 1846). Restrictions on young people's liberty may be put in place to remove them from situations of risk, including through secure or out-of-home care (explored in more detail later in this chapter). Unsurprisingly, young people who feel their privacy, concerns and interests are ignored in such situations may become angry, mistrustful and secretive. Practitioners may then find themselves in a 'double-bind', 'no-win' scenario, whereby attempts to protect 'might alienate a young person, paradoxically encouraging them to engage in further risky behaviours' (Lefevre et al, 2019: 1837).

Balancing welfare and criminal justice paradigms

Not all services have reached a point of foregrounding young people's vulnerability, care and protection in situations of EFRH. The recognition of exploitation when young people become involved in criminal activities such as drug dealing and violent extremism is still relatively recent. Aligned with the policy tensions detailed earlier, youth justice responses remain at the fore for these forms of EFRH, and young people in the UK can be incarcerated for their involvement in crime associated with experiences of abuse and exploitation. Wider attitudes towards young people tend towards suspicion and hostility, with an underpinning assumption that anti-social or criminal activity is involved when they occupy public spaces. This is particularly true for Black young people, who are increasingly losing all trust in statutory agencies, as their presence is vilified and controlled (Williams, 2018). This provides a disturbing wider context within which the highly intrusive internal search of 15-year-old Child Q for drugs, introduced at the outset of this chapter, is possible.

Some literature outside of the UK also expresses a need for systems that can protect young people who are both victims of and engage in harmful activity (Bruning and Doek, 2021). When young people occupy identities of both 'victim' and 'perpetrator', this can challenge how professional systems construct and respond to them. In the US, for instance, some state jurisdictions continue to criminalise victims of CSE and trafficking (Miller-Perrin and Wurtele, 2017; Pullmann et al, 2020). Young people are also drawn into the US juvenile justice system each year for 'status offences' – behaviours like truancy, underage drinking, running away and being beyond parental control – which (though not crimes) are prohibited because of a young person's status as a minor (Annie E. Casey Foundation, 2022). Even in European countries where youth justice systems have adopted a 'welfare' model, characterised by minimum intervention, education and restorative justice (Rap, 2015; Matthews et al, 2018), there is an apparent lack of protective responses to adolescents who are both victims of and engage in harmful activity, even where the latter results from experiences of exploitation or abuse.

Despite an increased framing in international guidance of child protection as a children's rights issue and increased focus on children's individual development needs and well-being (Gilbert et al, 2011; Spratt et al, 2014), responses to EFRH are not always welfare led and often remain situated outside child protection services. That is not to say that exploitation, peer abuse and so on do not offer the potential of serious harm for young people and other members of society, but rather to argue that practitioner and system responses that are 'done to' rather than 'with' young people are likely to be alienating and counterproductive in terms of decreasing risks to individuals and communities (Wroe and Lloyd, 2020).

Individualised or restrictive intervention models

A swing towards welfare-based responses to EFRH has seen social care organisations draw upon intervention models traditionally used in cases of familial abuse, such as out-of-home care, to safeguard young people who have been harmed beyond their family homes. Out-of-home care is used across a range of high-income countries for young people under 18 affected by CSE or trafficking. Placements include residential centres, group homes, secured or semi-secured facilities, or more temporary accommodations, such as hostels, emergency shelters or temporary reception centres.

Out-of-home care is used to remove young people from situations and contexts of risk, and/or to manage persistent episodes of them running away from home or care. Some placements in North America and Europe are referred to as 'specialised care provisions' for cases of exploitation or trafficking (Farrell et al, 2019; Organization for Security and Co-operation in Europe, 2019; Aussems et al, 2020), designed to engage with specific dynamics of EFRH and reduce the risk that being in care might exacerbate a young person's exposure to exploitation. However, some young people who have been sexually exploited or trafficked repeatedly go 'missing' from residential placements due to ongoing contact with those who exploit them. In some cases, placements or shelters have been targeted by those who exploit young people in North America (Werkmeister Rozas et al, 2018; Latzman et al, 2019), Australia (McKibbin and Humphreys, 2019) and Europe (Lumos, 2020). More broadly, the unsuitability and instability of placements can increase young people's (re-)exposure to EFRH (Palmer, 2019). There are also clear indications that safeguarding systems and practitioners in high-income countries continue to struggle to provide appropriate support in similar ways to the UK (Organization for Security and Co-operation in Europe, 2019; Palmer, 2019; Pullmann et al, 2020; The Economist Intelligence Unit, 2020). Child protection responses rarely go beyond interventions of one-to-one support for young people or offering parenting/family support to their carers (Radford et al, 2015; Okech et al, 2018; Benavente et al, 2021).

Despite these similarities, it should also be noted that in countries like Germany and Spain, and across Scandinavia, child protection systems are informed by social-pedagogical or ecological approaches (Grunwald and Thiersch, 2009; Hämäläinen, 2015). These approaches are centred on the importance of recognising and engaging with young people's social environments if their behaviours and experiences of harm and safety are to be understood. Compared to the UK, social work and youth work in countries influenced by these approaches tend to have stronger practice cultures of community-based interventions and group work – such as in Germany, with its well-established approach to 'mobile' or 'socio-spatial' youth work (Spatscheck and Wolf-Ostermann, 2009). However, as research into child protection responses to EFRH is so limited and the responses themselves are in such early development, there is little evidence on how these approaches may resolve the identified challenges of responding to EFRH.

Charting a way forward: the contribution of this book

In this book, we respond to the rapidly changing policy and practice landscape of the UK's approach to EFRH by outlining what is known to be effective or challenging about current social care responses to the issue. As highlighted in this introduction, while the policy developments and terminology applied in the UK are relatively unique, there is much about the challenges faced that crosses international boundaries. Neither the family-focused design of child protection systems, nor the practice challenges that come with safeguarding young people affected by EFRH, are the preserve of UK systems. As such, the findings presented in this book will be of relevance to a range of high-income countries in the Global North with an interest in offering welfare-oriented social care responses to EFRH.

The book is organised over eight further chapters that follow this introduction. Chapter Two outlines how our analysis of the literature on social care responses to EFRH led to a typology of five characteristics associated with promising or effective practice systems and methods. Chapters Three to Seven each present one of these five characteristics, focusing on what they may mean for the development and delivery of practice interventions with young people, as well the implications for whole-system or service design. Chapter Eight draws together the previous five chapters to offer a framework for designing policy and practice responses to EFRH in the future. In Chapter Nine, we reflect on what this framework suggests about the sufficiency of the UK policy and practice framework outlined in this introductory chapter, and recommend what may be required next to better respond to (and prevent) EFRH. We also use the closing chapter to raise questions for contexts beyond the UK where EFRH impacts young people, inviting researchers and policymakers in other settings to consider whether the systems they currently use are reflective of the framework produced through our review.

This book offers a conceptual framework to guide the design of services and systems that are used in response to EFRH. It serves as a central point of reference for those in the UK – noting where developments are already in place, as well as where system innovations (and improvement) are needed to ensure responses align with the evidence available. By offering a conceptual framework, this book also contributes to international debates about the safety of young people who are at risk of significant harm beyond their families. Young people can and do suffer significant harm in extra-familial contexts and relationships. We hope this book goes some way to ensuring that social care systems, both in the UK and beyond, can respond effectively when they do.

TWO

A framework for analysing the evidence

Introduction

Our review of the literature sought to identify and categorise the ways in which social care professionals and organisations respond to the EFRH encountered by young people in adolescence. To do so, we examined literature from countries with comparable child welfare systems to the UK that described and analysed discrete interventions and practice models or systemwide/whole-organisational approaches. In particular, our review considered how services and systems defined and measured effectiveness for any of these types of social care response, and what challenges there might be for practitioners and services when implementing them.

The review used the rapid evidence assessment method – an approach that enables a practical balance to be struck between rigour and resources when there is a need (as in this situation) for a timely synthesis of the available evidence base to inform the practice field (Crawford et al, 2015). This chapter briefly sets out the search and screening strategy, outlines the framework approach we took to analysis, and explores some of the definitional challenges of identifying and synthesising literature across countries that differ (often strongly) at a policy level in how they classify and direct responses to EFRH.

Further specific details of the methodology are available in the Appendix to this book. The chapter concludes with an integrated definition of EFRH and offers an approach to subcategorisation that illustrates where these forms of risk and harm vary and align.

Identifying relevant literature

The literature reviewed was located through a systematic search of four bibliographic databases, a public call for relevant materials through our academic and professional networks, and ongoing 'snowballing' from citations in publications already identified – these three methods in combination have been found to be most effective in reviews of complex and heterogeneous fields of evidence (Greenhalgh and Peacock, 2005). The data set included journal articles, research and evaluation reports (such as reports to funders), and policy or practice commentaries. We excluded any literature published prior to 2005 due to the rapidly changing public awareness of, and professional responses to, such harms as CSE from that time forward.

Our key inclusion criterion was that literature described or evaluated either practice interventions or whole-organisational and system approaches within social care services and settings that were designed to respond to EFRH experienced by young people in adolescence, whether as the sole focus or as part of a wider service. Much of the available literature discussing EFRH was not eligible for inclusion, as it centred on the dynamics of the harm and/or its impact on young people, rather than studying the interventions and services developed in response – unsurprising, perhaps, as this is an emergent field still poorly understood, particularly from the perspective of young people and their parents. Focusing the search entailed the combination of three terminological groupings. The first of these involved descriptors for children and young people. As we noted in Chapter One, we have applied a broad definition of adolescence (covering the ages of 12 to 25) to reflect how risk and vulnerability may continue into adulthood, and that services may need to bridge the transition between childhood and adulthood (Holmes and Smale, 2018). However, a large majority of the literature identified concerned young people within the 12 to 18 age bracket.

The second grouping of search terms covered types of EFRH, which we have defined as behaviours, relationships and activities engaged in, or encountered by, young people within peer, social and environmental contexts outside of the family home that are associated with exploitation or criminality, and where there is a clear or implied safeguarding concern (Firmin et al, 2019). Within this category are included: various forms of CSE and trafficking; criminal exploitation, including the form of drugs distribution called 'County Lines' in the UK (Hudek, 2018a); violence and abuse by peers and older adults, both singly and in groups, which may or may not occur within the context of an intimate relationship; 'gang' affiliation and other involvement in organised crime; and other forms of serious youth violence. We did also include radicalisation and violent extremism in the search, but very little could be found detailing services from a social care perspective, as opposed to criminal justice.

As there is no single term across the international literature that coalesces risks beyond the family home into a unified concept, our review strategy involved separate searches for each type of harm, using a range of terminologies for similar or overlapping forms of behaviour, relationships and crime. Also, whereas England, Wales and Scotland increasingly recognises and links EFRH to national child protection and wider safeguarding policies (Her Majesty's Government, 2018; Stanley, 2020; Scottish Government, 2021; Welsh Government, 2021), within most other countries, no such integration is apparent. We noted, for example, that the trafficking of minors was discussed discretely from safeguarding considerations, even for young people under the age of majority.

The third grouping in our search strategy encompassed terms for interventions, practice models and whole-organisational or system approaches responding to EFRH within the social care field. Like EFRH, 'social care' is not a term with international salience. Within the UK, it includes social work, safeguarding and other services related to the care, protection or social or emotional support of children and young people who would be at risk of harm without them (SCIE, 2012). In this book, we have extended this broad definition to cover services and interventions delivered by organisations and practitioners within statutory, voluntary (non-profit) and community sectors to respond to EFRH. Types of response encompassed by this review included: proactive and preventive strategies to address potential risk at a cohort level, such as school-wide psycho-educational programmes; targeted interventions for young people already involved in risky or harmful relationships and situations; and whole-system configurations within or across organisations. While we screened in studies of interagency responses that included social care as a key partner, we excluded numerous studies that were primarily about the response of another agency (often criminal justice, education or health).

Each publication considered for inclusion was further screened for methodological rigour and only included if it featured a clear methodological account. We further screened for rigour at the point of applying the framework analysis to establish the quality of the findings associated with the key themes, including whether they were extracted from randomised controlled trials, quasi-experimental studies, evidence reviews, small qualitative studies or process evaluations. In Chapter Four, for example, we note that the majority of literature on the importance of improving multi-agency collaboration derives from inquiries and commissioned policy reports from the UK, though this theme was more generally supported by a range of research papers in the data set.

Analysing and categorising

A total of 126 items remained in our final data set for analysis, including empirically based journal articles, research and evaluation reports (such as reports to funders), and policy or practice commentaries. Given the relatively large size of this data set, we applied a framework analysis approach (Ritchie et al, 2003). This involved identifying measures of effectiveness, intended outcomes, criticisms and challenges for each social care response, and looking for patterns and associations. Early on in the process, we identified that the broad set of responses described or evaluated in our data set did not share a singular definition of effectiveness: in short, they were trying to achieve a range of diverse aims or intended results. For example, where a service was introducing a new system approach, the focus of the report was on process (a more efficient system), rather than end outcomes for young people. As such, rather than apply a discrete definition of effectiveness to the literature, we looked for evidence in each source that the effectiveness of the response had been considered in a meaningful way for that context. Patterns and associations identified in the literature were then grouped into subthemes and gradually built into an overarching set of descriptive categories of social care responses to EFRH.

Building a thematic framework

Each paper was analysed to establish the quality of evidence for the various approaches to EFRH and coded according to the following questions:

- What were the objectives of the professional response that has been studied or evaluated?
- Were any positive outcomes found? If yes, what were they, and how robust was the evidence?
- What were the study's limitations?

- What challenges had services experienced in implementing their organisational or practice responses to EFRH?
- Were there any criticisms by the authors of the approach taken?
- What did authors recommend in light of their analyses?

The answers to these research questions were used to develop a thematic explanatory account of the approaches that had formed, and the challenges faced by professionals, in responding to EFRH, as well as to identify thematic recommendations related to future practice interventions and organisational or system approaches that offered promise. Themes within and across all questions were grouped into subthemes and gradually into larger themes using a framework approach. The relative strength of a theme was then categorised as either 'strong' or 'clear'. If 10–20 per cent of the literature featured the theme, we considered this a *clear* theme. If over 20 per cent of the literature featured that theme, we classified it as *strong*. Only clear or strong thematic findings have been used to construct the typology outlined in this book and the framework for improving and transforming services that it builds towards, which is set out in Chapter Eight.

Characteristics of effective or promising social care responses

This iterative approach to framework analysis enabled us to discern five clear or strong themes that characterised promising or effective practice interventions or organisational/system responses to EFRH:

- interventions and systems that draw on, or aim to build, relationships between young people and protective adults (including professionals, foster carers and family members);
- intra- and inter-organisational structures and policies directed towards improving interagency working and ensuring that systems are implemented to best effect;

- approaches that seek to change the context(s) within which EFRH occurs and any associated structural drivers;
- systems or interventions that address the specific dynamics of EFRH, rather than generalist approaches focusing on or within the family; and
- a youth-centred service ethos that takes into account the dynamics of adolescence when tailoring the service to ensure it is both relevant for and accessible to young people.

Clustering types of harm

Our initial stages of analysis suggested that while it was possible to identify clear or strong themes across our sample, some were more strongly associated with some forms of EFRH than others. Given the complexity of the task at hand and the potential pitfalls of grouping together such a broad and somewhat disparate set of publications, we further analysed the themes identified by subtypes of EFRH. To do this, we streamlined the key mechanisms or contexts of EFRH into five clusters of harm type: harm involving peers; sexual harm; harm associated with criminality; harm via exploitation; and radicalisation. Each mechanism or context of EFRH was mapped to one or more of these clusters (outlined in Table 2.1). Through this mapping, it was notable that some of the clusters had 'fuzzy' rather than clear-cut boundaries (Alexander and Enns, 1988); while they share similar central tendencies or associated features, there are overlaps in how they might be experienced by young people and what they require from professional or organisational responses. Sexual exploitation, for example, can share many dynamics of manipulation, threat and grooming with criminal exploitation, but it may also overlap with other forms of sexual abuse. To account for this fuzziness, some mechanisms of EFRH were coded in more than one cluster.

Examining the strength of identified themes by harm-type cluster allowed us to further assess the results of the framework

Table 2.1: Harm-type clusters

Key mechanism or context of the EFRH	Clusters of harm type					
	Harm via peers	Harm via sexual abuse	Harm via criminality	Harm via exploitation	Harm via radicalisation	
Serious youth violence, including knife crime	X					
Peer-to-peer abuse (various/generic)	X					
Harmful sexual behaviour	X	X				
Partner violence (peer-to-peer)	X					
Peer-to-peer abuse (sexual violence)	X	X				
Suicide	X					
CSE		X		X		
Child sexual abuse (general)		X				
Sexual violence (not by peer)		X				
Child criminal exploitation			X	X		
County Lines, other drugs distribution or 'cuckooing'			X	X		

Key mechanism or context of the EFRH	Clusters of harm type					
	Harm via peers	Harm via sexual abuse	Harm via criminality	Harm via exploitation	Harm via radicalisation
Crime but not necessarily harm			X		
Modern slavery			X	X	
Gang affiliation			X		
Trafficking				X	X
Radicalisation					X
Violent extremism					X

analysis and the extent to which characteristics of social care responses to EFRH held true for all types of harm included in this broad category.

The types of EFRH discussed in the literature had been categorised within five harm-type clusters: EFRH via peers, EFRH via exploitation, EFRH via criminality, EFRH via sexual abuse and EFRH via radicalisation. Two subgroupings of the harm-type clusters became apparent through this: EFRH involving criminality or peers; and EFRH involving exploitation or sexual abuse (see Figure 2.1). Analysing the five characteristics of promising or effective social care responses with reference to the harm-type clusters, it emerged that the recommended focus of interventions, as well as where they were most challenging to implement, differed markedly between each of the two subgroupings. Relational approaches to practice were more readily recommended in the literature on EFRH involving exploitation or sexual abuse, whereas contextual approaches, and the challenges of structural harm, were stronger characteristics of responses to address EFRH involving criminality or peers. Moreover, approaches that improved the implementation of existing systems (particularly in respect of multi-agency working) proved a stronger theme for responding to EFRH involving exploitation or sexual abuse, whereas a need for system or legislative reforms limited the extent to which improving multi-agency working was recommended for EFRH involving criminality or peers. Given that some forms of EFRH were more represented in the data set than others, these two variations should be treated with caution. Nonetheless, they do indicate substantial differences in how social care services respond to different forms of EFRH, possibly relating to some of the conceptual and policy drivers that were noted in Chapter One, and questions are raised for how organisations and interventions should be structured if they are to be effective and responsive to young people across these harm types. We will discuss these throughout each ensuing chapter and return to this point in Chapter Eight.

Figure 2.1: Typology of social care responses to EFRH

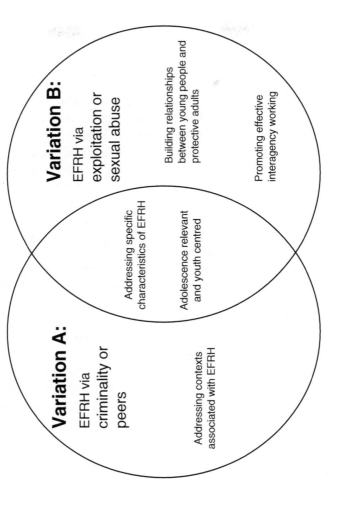

Variation A:

EFRH via criminality or peers

Addressing contexts associated with EFRH

Addressing specific characteristics of EFRH

Adolescence relevant and youth centred

Variation B:

EFRH via exploitation or sexual abuse

Building relationships between young people and protective adults

Promoting effective interagency working

A note on the limitations of this review

It is important to note some of the limitations of this review. The 'rapid' nature of our methodology meant that our search was not exhaustive. We searched only four databases and did not manually search all journals that might have included relevant literature. Our sample was also limited to publications in English. Although we sought to identify studies or descriptions of social care responses in countries beyond the UK that had relatively comparable welfare and safeguarding systems, substantially more literature from the UK context was identified and included. While we did include publications focused on young adults in the 18- to 25-year-old category, we filtered out studies examining responses to adults more broadly as opposed to young people. This means that we are likely to have omitted relevant literature relating to older adolescents and, with this, practice responses that address transitions to adulthood. By prioritising papers that were more likely to report 'social care' responses (social work, multi-agency responses and the voluntary sector), we likely excluded papers covering responses from other sectors (such as health and criminal justice agencies) that may have surfaced results relevant to the themes identified. Finally, our review focused on broad themes, connections and differences within a relatively large and complex group of literature, and so we have not captured in our analysis every reason for effectiveness, recommendation, criticism or challenge covered by a study.

Moving forward

Over the next five chapters, we will analyse the research evidence for the five characteristics that are associated with promise or effectiveness in our typology of social care responses to EFRH. In Chapter Eight, we then synthesise these analyses, noting where recommendations converge or differ for each harm type and the two subgroupings (involving criminality/

peers or exploitation/sexual abuse) in order to construct a framework for understanding and improving responses to EFRH. We end, in Chapter Nine, with overarching reflections on the implications of our review for future policy, practice and research, both within the UK and beyond.

THREE

Building relationships

Introduction

Positive relationships with adults who have their best interests at heart can be a significant protective factor in enabling children and young people to safely navigate risky relationships and situations outside of their home and family. The first of the promising or effective professional responses to EFRH detailed within our typology concerns interventions and systems that draw on, or aim to build, relationships between young people and protective adults. It is increasingly recognised that it is not only relationships with parents, other family members and formal caregivers that can confer such benefits, but also those with professionals and other adults within the community.

Three kinds of relationship emerged most strongly in the literature as having a clear benefit for addressing EFRH. The strongest body of evidence supported the building of *trusted relationships* between professionals and young people facing EFRH. Numerous studies also highlighted the importance of a *collaborative relationship* between professionals and either young people in these situations or their parents/carers. Finally, a smaller set of sources examined efforts to foster or utilise wider *community relationships* – including with local businesses, schools and charitable organisations – to build networks of support for young people and families affected by EFRH. In this chapter, we outline how these three kinds of relationship might be harnessed as an intervention, as a route to enhancing the effectiveness of practice approaches or to underpin systemwide/whole-organisational approaches to EFRH.

Building trusted relationships between young people and professionals

Sources from a range of countries and different practice contexts reached a similar conclusion: relationships of trust between young people and professionals are a key feature of building effective responses to EFRH (Kohli et al, 2015; McGuire, 2018; National Youth Agency, 2020). Mechanisms that facilitate young people's relationships with protective adults were the most common feature of effective organisational or systemwide approaches to addressing EFRH, and almost one fifth of services discussed in that literature were intending to further develop or enhance the relational features of their approach in the future. Relational working was also the second-most common feature of practice interventions thought to be effective in addressing EFRH.

In order to understand why relational principles are so central to effective professional responses to EFRH, it is necessary to recognise first how prior experiences of abuse, exploitation or other forms of developmental trauma have affected young people's sense of self, resilience in situations of risk and capacity to trust others (Ofsted, 2011). Developmental psychology literature indicates that children need sufficiently safe, nurturing and reliable caregiving as they grow up to develop secure attachments and the associated capacity to think reflectively and emotionally self-regulate; when this has been less than optimal, they may depend more on external validation for their self-worth and seek out unsafe sources of comfort and distraction when they are anxious or distressed (Hickle and Lefevre, 2022). As they move into adolescence, young people's prior experiences of neglect, abuse, exploitation and betrayal may mean that they are less prepared to confide in others or to expect that they will be cared about, respected, believed and protected; all this may translate into a reduced capacity to identify, avoid or withstand coercive and exploitative social situations and intimate relationships (McGuire, 2018). Abusive peers and adults will capitalise on such vulnerabilities in the targeting and grooming process, and commonly seek to further undermine a young person's existing relationships with family, friends and professionals in order to better isolate and manipulate them (Hallett, 2015).

Prioritising or foregrounding the establishment of a trusting relationship can increase the likelihood that a young person will engage in an intervention. It can also provide a form of therapeutic repair. For example, the relational approach of an adolescent leadership development programme in the US for African American youths living in areas with high levels of street violence was able to enhance their:

> internal foundations for their future professional and personal relationships. ... The youth talked about the transformative nature of relationships, describing how their capacity for more intimate, attuned relationships increased during their time in the program. Consider Lenny who said, 'Because, at first before the social worker stuff, I didn't really care too much about what other people thought.' (Bulanda and McCrea, 2013: 111)

Person-centred qualities were mentioned time and again across the studies we reviewed, for example, being friendly, relatable, empathic, relaxed and non-judgemental, and showing unconditional positive regard (Sturrock, 2012; Countryman-Roswurm and Bolin, 2014; Bounds et al, 2020). A 21-year-old young woman involved with the Safe Choices Leaving Care and Custody Project Programme on Sexual Exploitation described the impact of her worker's approach:

I don't know why, but I feel comfortable. It makes it easy as I don't have to explain why things happen, she explains to other professionals. Some people you know are judging you, but she doesn't. ... I've never found anything she's kept from me, whereas for other professionals, I have. [Worker] is the only one I can trust out of all the professionals. (Quoted in Coy, 2017: 3)

Where professionals sustained a relationship over time, young people could begin (perhaps for the first time) to experience reliability and predictability (Bulanda and McCrea, 2013; Boulton et al, 2019). Two pilot programmes in response to CSE in the UK found that professionals who were persistent in 'sticking with' a young person – remaining present if things went wrong or progress was hampered, even if the young person avoided or rejected contact with them initially – gave children a sense that they were worthy of care and respect (Shuker, 2015; Scott et al, 2017b). Also in the UK, workers in the Safe Choices – Leaving Care and Custody programme for young women facing sexual exploitation and violence in the context of gang association reported that being able to extend support for as long as was needed was crucial to achieving the project aims (Coy, 2017).

However, other studies suggested that flexibility in the type, intensity and length of a relationship might be as important as its potential to be sustained (Hudek, 2018b). Ad hoc availability of professionals when needed was an important dimension of trust building:

[My worker is] someone I can trust. That's the first thing that comes to mind. And someone I class as a friend and he doesn't need to be a friend, but he acts like a friend anyway. No it's his job. This is his job. He doesn't have to answer the phone to give me advice at silly o'clock but he does. He's there when I need him. (Sturrock, 2012: 69)

Other young people affected by EFRH preferred brief or crisis-led support, and this could be effective in certain situations too. Fagan and Catalano's (2013) review of violence reduction programmes in North America found that some relatively short-term but intensive therapeutic interventions produced effects lasting for a number of years. At a broader level, practice interventions involving a fixed number of weeks/days or predefined tasks may be less suitable to facilitating relationships of trust than those with more flexibility.

To be persistent, caring, flexible and creative in their interventions, practitioners need time to plan their work, get to know the young person and be able to go at their pace. Hudek's (2018b) study of a UK response to young people who were being criminally exploited found that practitioners in the voluntary (non-profit) and community sector were more likely to have time for the intensive work needed to engage young people and create change. However, where statutory social care organisations were able to reduce caseloads for staff engaged in EFRH work, this made a big difference (Scott et al, 2017a). A number of studies recognised that working through empathic, emotionally attuned and responsive relationships with young people who may be traumatised, distressed, angry and hostile can be overwhelming and stressful (Coy, 2017; Scott et al, 2017a). A UK-based study by the second author of this book, considering system and practice responses to CSE in three regions, highlighted reflective individual and group supervision as a crucial tool for validating and processing the emotional labour and psychological impact of this work, enabling professionals to practise sensitively and effectively (Lefevre et al, 2017).

Building working alliances with young people, parents and carers

Aside from trusting relationships, the second-most common way in which practitioners in the studies reviewed were able to engage young people in productive interventions was through collaborative relationships. Such 'working alliances' were facilitated by an atmosphere of 'mutual respect' and the establishment of 'agreed goals' (Sturrock, 2012: 74). Young people described how they needed to feel involved rather than 'done to' (Thomas and D'Arcy, 2017; Child Safeguarding Practice Review Panel, 2020). A commitment to collaborative working was demonstrated by professionals involving young people in decisions about interventions (Bulanda and McCrea, 2013; Public Health England, 2020) or offering young people opportunities to participate in designing interventions or support plans (Anderson and Parkinson, 2018; Van de Vijver and Harvey, 2019). It was notable that references to these principles proliferated in studies examining practice interventions but were much less obvious in organisational or whole-system approaches to addressing EFRH.

Both young people and their parents often feel frightened of, or hostile towards, professionals in situations of authority (especially in statutory agencies), not only because of earlier experiences of trauma and abuse, but also due to prior or current experiences of powerlessness (Berelowitz et al, 2015; Shuker, 2018). Practitioners in voluntary sector support and intervention programmes often enjoyed the advantage of being seen as more independent (Hudek, 2018b; Kohli et al, 2015). However, professionals acknowledging power differentials and ensuring transparent communication were important starting points in any setting (Beatriz et al, 2018).

Practice interventions that facilitated collaborative relationships with parents or carers were better able to build and utilise their strengths as active partners in safety planning for young people affected by EFRH. Once parents were 'invited to be experts' about their children and felt that they were respected as members of the intervention team, joint working towards shared goals became more possible (Van de Vijver and Harvey, 2019). This required professionals sharing their ideas without adopting a position of expertise or blame, especially as parents had often felt that they were held responsible for their child's exposure to EFRH (Scott et al, 2017b). A number of UK-based papers reported how specialist training, wider intensive support or advocacy were used to support parents' and foster carers' understanding of the nature of CSE and how it might impact the behaviour of their children (Shuker, 2015; Scott et al, 2017a; Pike et al, 2019). Such responses were built on the idea that if parents/carers are well informed, for example, about the dynamics of grooming, they can work more effectively alongside professionals in the safeguarding endeavour.

Collaborative working also creates the conditions in which parents/carers can repair their own relationships with their children – relationships that have often been compromised, or put under additional strain, as a result of both EFRH and subsequent service interventions. This is important as improved parent–child relationships have been found to be protective against future exploitation (Thomas and D'Arcy, 2017; Pike et al, 2019). A US-based family intervention to reduce risk factors for sexual exploitation included mediation between family members to address this directly (Bounds et al, 2020).

Developing community and wider networks of relational support

There are some indications that relationships with benign or supportive adults, such as volunteers and non-professional community practitioners who are part of young people's networks beyond the home and family, can also offer potential avenues for strengths building and safeguarding from EFRH. Trust, again, is an underpinning principle. However, the factors that characterise 'trusted' community relationships are somewhat different to those identified for relationships between young people and professionals. Relationships developed in young people's own social contexts are more often experienced as enduring, authentic or reliable: where adults involved are from young people's local communities, they are considered more capable of understanding the realities of young people's lives; as they are involved without being paid, young people may feel that they have their best interests at heart; and, finally, as their involvement is not because of EFRH, young people may be less concerned that they will disappear if and when the EFRH ends (Bulanda and McCrea, 2013; Miller et al, 2013; Bounds et al, 2020; National Youth Agency, 2020; Wroe and Lloyd, 2020). Some studies reviewed suggested that professionals might also benefit from building relationships with community organisations and residents in areas with a prevalence of EFRH to better understand the specific nature of risks in that area and extend their capacity to reach affected young people (D'Arcy and Thomas, 2016).

School-based interventions comprised an important subset of this literature, with after-school programmes occupying a relational middle space between formal services and informal community networks. Using principles of relational and collaborative intervention, they offer opportunities for professionals to build trust and engagement with young people, thus allowing young people to experience professional adults in a positive light (Bulanda and McCrea, 2013; Matthews et al, 2018). Establishing or reinforcing relationships between *parents* and schools may also offer important opportunities. Letourneau et al (2017) discuss how in whole-school interventions in the US to reduce incidents of harmful sexual behaviour, mutually reinforcing relationships between schools and parents help to create a seamless set of consistent messages for young people, both in and outside of education.

Conclusion

Our review identified a body of literature that revealed relational and collaborative strategies as both an established and somewhat emergent feature of organisational and practice responses to EFRH. There is clear evidence that trusted relationships with social care professionals can enhance young people's engagement in services, increasing the likelihood that they will share their views and experiences, and more readily utilise available forms of help. There is also some evidence that relational approaches may be therapeutic in themselves, boosting young people's resilience to future risk through helping repair some of the vulnerabilities caused by earlier developmental trauma. The features that characterise such relationships, their role in systems and interventions, and the conditions in which they flourish are varied. This variation is informed both by the organisational setting of professionals (voluntary, independent or statutory) and by the needs of a young person at a given time (for proactive and sustained or reactive and short-term work).

To a lesser extent, practice interventions have sought to build collaborative relationships between professionals and parents/ carers, and, through this, to nurture young people's relationships with their parents/carers. While young people clearly value relationships with non-professional adults – particularly those based in the social contexts where they spend their time – the extent to which these relationships are understood/valued in the context of EFRH is very much emergent.

Our analysis of this body of literature suggests that all these forms of relationship are interwoven and have the potential to mutually reinforce each other towards safeguarding young people affected by EFRH. However, it also appears that the practice or community conditions required for such relationships to flourish are yet to be firmly established, involving substantial resource challenges in situations of constrained public finances.

FOUR

Improving interagency collaboration

Introduction

The second characteristic of promising or effective professional responses to EFRH set out within our typology concerns the development of intra- and inter-organisational structures and policies that are directed towards improving interagency working. Although our review was focused on social care responses to EFRH, a number of publications discussed these in the context of wider safeguarding, child protection, child welfare and crime-reduction-focused partnerships. While the roles of a number of different agencies were discussed within this literature – including community organisations, health agencies and schools – it was the relationship between social care and policing organisations that was most commonly the centre of focus.

The need to improve interagency working was particularly highlighted within UK publications, but sources from a range of countries noted both that EFRH could not be adequately addressed without interagency collaboration and that struggles to form effective partnerships were a persistent challenge. In this chapter, we detail the steps social care organisations have taken to improve interagency working, and in considering some of the challenges identified in the literature, we reflect upon whether present approaches and ambitions are sufficient. In particular, we note that partners have often used protocols, processes and procedures to foster effective interagency responses to EFRH, but we question whether these activities have created the common sense of purpose that appears to be required.

Partnerships, processes and protocols

Enhanced collaboration between professionals or across services was defined as increasing the effectiveness of responses to EFRH in 15 per cent of the subgroup of literature covering organisational and system developments. McKibbin and Humphreys (2019: 427) in Australia, for example, conclude that 'the best available evidence indicates that multiagency collaboration involving the police, government and community service organisations provides the most robust response to sexual exploitation'. For much of this literature, increased effectiveness was defined as approaches that built a shared or common understanding of EFRH, facilitated coordinated practice responses across disparate agencies, or ensured that a range of resources were coordinated around a shared need.

Perhaps unsurprisingly, given the co-dependency between agencies involved in tackling EFRH, activities undertaken to improve collaboration in these settings were often process or structure driven. In England, for example, statutory guidance issued in 2009 directed towards the newly recognised safeguarding implications of CSE recommended multidisciplinary subgroupings to bring together professionals (particularly from social care, health and the police) so as to coordinate interventions (Department for Children, Schools and Families, 2009). Dedicated multi-agency teams and units have been a prevalent model for responding to EFRH in the UK since that time and are frequently cited as a major contributory factor to effective responses, as they facilitate the development of shared understandings, cultures, protocols to govern shared practices and formal agreements for how information might be shared between organisations (Frost, 2017). A large-scale study involving a survey of 144 local safeguarding children boards in England, interviews with 104 practitioners in 24 areas and analysis of 1,065 case files of young people found that physically co-locating such teams was the most effective model for developing the kind of close working relationships that enable practitioners to share information effectively and develop a mutual understanding of each other's capabilities, capacity and working practices (Jago et al, 2011). As one practitioner commented: 'the only way you get that leap is through these specialist teams, when you're sitting in one another's seats all day' (Jago et al, 2011: 39). This is important, as the absence of such mutual and transparent practices has frequently been noted in the UK where a young person has died or experienced serious harm, and the inadequate professional response prior to this was thought to play a contributory role (Sidebotham et al, 2016; Brandon et al, 2020). As a result, the enhanced sharing of information and 'decisive, multi-agency intervention' have been proposed as national policy objectives in an independent review of children's social care in England, including where there is risk of exploitation: 'Strong multi-agency working means that services and decisions are joined up and focused on what is best for children and families' (MacAlister, 2022: 197–8). The benefits of avoiding duplication when services are co-located were also noted, not only for practitioners, but also for young people and families, who found it easier and less confusing to access services when they were all in one place.

Whether through formal units or looser virtual groupings, the aim of multi-agency collaborations is not to lose or blur the distinct contribution that different agencies can offer in terms of their disciplinary knowledge or specific role responses, but rather to create a single, mutually agreed set of aims, values, pathways and procedures, so that practices are consistent in both process and how they are experienced by young people and families. In a 2016 study of how ten local authorities in England were responding to young people who were at risk of radicalisation, a key factor in improving practice was found to be the development of a single referral process, supported by shared procedural documents and tailored training materials. These facilitated professionals in reaching a consensus around shared definitions of this emergent threat and the extent to which it represents a safeguarding or child protection risk (Chisholm and Coulter, 2017).

It was noteworthy that the literature in our sample recommending how improving interagency working could lead to more effective practice derived predominantly from studies or practice reviews conducted within UK (and largely English) contexts. Many of the sources were produced by regulators (Ofsted, 2011; Ofsted et al, 2018) or practice associations (ADCS, 2019), or came from inquiries into the sufficiency of local responses (Scotland's Commissioner for Children and Young People, 2011; All-Party Parliamentary Group for Runaway and Missing Children and Adults, 2017). Their findings do, though, echo messages from the wider body of research from the UK and beyond that has reported on the process and impact of efforts to improve partnership working. Across these publications, we found both efforts to create interagency working through strategies and streamlined processes, and challenges in their *consistent and effective* implementation – challenges that are identified both within and outside the UK.

Challenges of interagency working: inconsistency and discord

Such challenges with interagency working were reported in almost one fifth of the literature covering organisational or system responses to EFRH. These challenges could be divided into two similar-sized groups: the first were challenges in effectively, and consistently, coordinating activity between professionals; and the second related to instances where the remit of different professionals/organisations within a partnership was disputed or unclear.

Challenges in coordinating different partner organisations in response to EFRH were identified in Australia (McKibbin and Humphreys, 2019), the US (Liles et al, 2016) and in a global review of organisational responses (Muraya and Fry, 2016), as well as dominating UK reviews, inquiries and discussion papers (Scotland's Commissioner for Children and Young People, 2011; Ofsted, 2011, 2019; Association of Directors of Children's Services, 2019). Many instances of what was happening in practice settings were the converse illustrations of the activities associated with effective practice outlined earlier. Efforts in the UK to coordinate activities between agencies, for example, were sometimes hampered by limited information sharing between agencies (Berelowitz et al, 2015; Mason-Jones and Loggie, 2020), whereas practice promoting young people's safety and wider welfare has been found to be facilitated by the kind of transparent and streamlined information-sharing procedures referenced earlier. Muraya and Fry (2016), when reviewing services offered to child sex-trafficking victims globally, found that such challenges were exacerbated when each agency within a partnership used separate case management systems or followed organisational, rather than shared, processes to guide their response. In short, not only did coordination and consistency appear to be hampered by an absence of the policies, processes and protocols outlined earlier in this chapter, but even when protocols were available, such as England's safeguarding guidance on CSE, they were also not always applied consistently (Pearce, 2014).

A further challenge identified in our review sheds partial light on why. Multiple publications surfaced tensions in agreeing what the remit of social care and/or wider partners should be when responding to EFRH. A total of 12 studies from UK contexts alone provided examples of how such roles had been disputed. Some reported that local authority social workers struggled to understand the focus of their role in responding to EFRH in situations where families were protective of (and not contributing to the harm experienced by) young people (Lloyd and Firmin, 2020). A lack of understanding about how young people are caught up in new and evolving threats, and the harmful impacts that are caused for them, adds to this uncertainty about roles (Chisholm and Coulter, 2017).

Other authors identified a lack of clarity about the role of the police in responding to EFRH – particularly in how welfare oriented they should be in their responses to the young people affected given their primary role focus on law enforcement and criminal justice (Ofsted et al, 2018; Turner et al, 2019). In situations where young people are both offending and being victimised simultaneously (explored in more detail in Chapter Eight), the tensions generated by different agency perspectives on the most appropriate response come to the fore. If the remit of the police is to investigate and prove crimes, which crimes should they prioritise in cases of EFRH – those *by* young people or those *against* young people – and is there agreement about such matters across a partnership (Turner et al, 2019)? Leaving these tensions unresolved creates space in which increased interagency working, such as effective information sharing, may increase police oversight of young people experiencing EFRH without sufficient safeguards that this will not result in their criminalisation (Williams, 2018; Wroe, 2021).

Such challenges were not solely found within and across statutory agencies. A number of publications have noted the important role that the voluntary sector can play in addressing EFRH (Leon and Raws, 2016). Yet, as statutory agencies have become increasingly involved in responding to EFRH over the past decade, the role of voluntary organisations has often been less clear, chiming with the gaps found in relationships between community members and statutory professionals documented in Chapter Three. A report on youth agencies' responses to 'gangs' and exploitation in England, for example, noted that the contribution of youth workers to creating safety in extra-familial contexts had been overlooked and undervalued in developing professional responses in the context of COVID-19 (National Youth Agency, 2020). Following a three-year evaluation of 13 CSE services in England, Shuker (2018) concluded that the distinctive and relevant contribution that voluntary sector services can make to the development of multi-agency plans, processes and structures, as well as their capacity to engage vulnerable and mistrustful children and young people, meant that the voluntary sector should be routinely involved in formal safeguarding arrangements.

Shared activities or shared goals?

Given the challenges outlined earlier, it is somewhat unsurprising that a subset of the UK publications reviewed ($n = 14$) criticised some organisations for not working effectively alongside others to fulfil their duties to safeguard young people affected by EFRH. Despite various policy developments and campaigns in the UK, some practitioners struggle when communicating with young people and misunderstand, or are unable to recognise, the signs of sexual exploitation (Mason-Jones and Loggie, 2020). When young people are also engaged in offending behaviours, their vulnerability or victimhood with reference to EFRH is not always prioritised and a criminal justice agenda may dominate interagency professional responses (Cockbain and Brayley, 2012; Astrup, 2019). Participants in a mixed-methods study of criminal exploitation involving 151 local authorities and 32 police forces in England and Wales commented on the different views and attitudes about choice and agency that may affect collaboration:

> I think that we struggle a lot with children's social care, social workers and the police ... there's still this perception that in some cases it is a choice and the young person is offending through choice and that's a daily struggle for us. ...

> there's something automatically in terms of people's internal value base that say they're less deserving because they're already involved in crime. (Turner et al, 2019: 71)

Attitudes towards race, gender or sexuality can also prevent practitioners from recognising exploitation and peer-to-peer sexual abuse (Leon and Raws, 2016; Clements et al, 2017; Lloyd et al, 2020). It seems that processes and protocols alone have not fostered a shared understanding of the different forms of EFRH – nor, importantly, a shared approach to responding.

When making recommendations for developing future practice, nearly one quarter of the organisational literature recommended one of two ways to improve interagency working in response to EFRH: building a common purpose among individuals and organisations; or improving professional understanding of, and practice approaches to, EFRH. One hot point of dissonance was the differing views that often emerged between agencies about the extent to which young people made 'choices' about their involvement in exploitation. Studies in the US (Sapiro et al, 2016), the UK (Reisel, 2017) and Australia (McKibbin and Humphreys, 2019) of young people going missing from home or care in the context of CSE all recommended that partner agencies develop a shared understanding of adolescent agency and vulnerability to facilitate more cohesive interagency responses. The introduction of peer support structures, so that practitioners could work together, and reflect on their practice, in what can be a challenging and highly pressurised field of work, was another promising mechanism (Clements et al, 2017; Lefevre et al, 2019). In this sense, a common purpose or shared goal could be built over time and reflected on in an iterative and active rather than static and policy-based fashion.

Cross-agency training was recommended in numerous publications to help practitioners work more collectively and consistently across the different agency systems when responding to EFRH. Most such recommendations were drawn from studies of CSE responses, for example, in enabling practitioners to develop mutual ways of recognising and responding to the multi-factorial and complex nature of CSE (Ofsted, 2015; Mason-Jones and Loggie, 2020). This perhaps reflected the greater length of time since the recognition of this phenomenon, and the accumulation of an increasing body of knowledge, compared with other more recently emergent forms of EFRH. There were clear indications that co-training could improve shared recognition of CSE in the following areas: that among boys and young men; that among young people with disabilities; the links between adolescent neglect and experiences of CSE; the identification of when there was an absence of consent; and regarding what constitutes abuse in cases of peer-instigated CSE (Leon and Raws, 2016; Franklin and Smeaton, 2017). Findings from a small study in England of decision making in CSE cases involving ten practitioners and managers from social work, youth work, family support and youth-offending work led Reisel (2017) to propose training scenarios using vignettes that would enable professionals to explore together pivotal moments in young people's lives that had influenced the future direction of the CSE they were experiencing, deepening their understandings of young people's constrained agency from a range of perspectives. Calls to implement existing guidance to better effect often accompanied training recommendations in these studies, suggesting that effective responses were possible in situations of EFRH but had not always been mobilised.

Building a common purpose

Our review indicated that many responses to EFRH, particularly in the UK, are designed and delivered through interagency partnerships, formed either across statutory services or between statutory and voluntary agencies. Interdisciplinary and inter-sector partnerships that were characterised by shared understandings, cultures and protocols seemed better prepared and more confident in how they should assess and address EFRH, but these did not necessarily resolve the challenges that were experienced in system implementation or practice response. Across the body of literature, researchers identified professionals who encountered difficulties either when drawing on established partnerships (such as between police and social care) or when having to establish new partnerships (between social care and community organisations, for example) to better address contemporary harms.

In the UK, the role of social care within such partnerships, and the role of those partnerships in supporting social care, has been principally developed through the introduction of various interagency processes and policies. However, the introduction of partnership frameworks appears to have been insufficient for facilitating meaningful interagency responses to EFRH. EFRH requires agencies to work to a shared goal that is not only underdeveloped in its scope and vision, but may also be contrary to their own individual agency goals or desired outcomes. Creating shared understandings of EFRH and revisiting the role of each agency when responding to this harm type (as opposed to familial abuse, for example) may offer some routes to working towards this common purpose. Without it, interagency responses to EFRH (and the social of social care within them) may be challenged for some time to come.

FIVE

Changing contexts of harm

Introduction

The third characteristic of effective professional responses detailed within our typology was drawn from organisational and practice literature revealing a need for the contextual and structural drivers of EFRH to be considered and engaged with by social care if young people's safeguarding and wider welfare needs are to be adequately addressed. Practice interventions, in particular, were found to be more effective at identifying and addressing sources of harm, when this was the case. Yet, it was the absence, rather than the presence, of such work, and the impact of this, that was most often noted within the literature.

In this chapter, we discuss some of the ways in which social care services have successfully engaged with peer, school and (to a lesser extent) community settings associated with EFRH to improve young people's well-being and safety. We then highlight how structural factors, such as poverty, racism and sexism, appear to undermine the efficacy of interventions and organisational responses if their effects remain unaddressed, and note recommendations made regarding potential useful approaches. We close the chapter by outlining the shortcomings of social care responses directed towards the promotion of social order and cohesion (Payne, 2020), that is, where the goal of intervention is to enable individual young people to resolve problems, adapt and conform, rather than additionally or alternatively seeking to change social structures or systems that produce harm or perpetuate risk for young people as a whole.

Responding to peer, school, and community contexts

The review identified clear evidence in over one third (35 per cent) of the interventions literature that social care may effectively enhance safety for young people where it is able to directly address risk dynamics in the places, groups and other environments where young people are experiencing harm or becoming involved with dangerous or criminal activities. Interventions that proactively and pre-emptively seek to increase mechanisms for safety in the schools, peer relationships or community settings where young people spend their time are also associated with reducing future risk of EFRH.

School-based interventions commonly seek to address EFRH through proactively changing cultural norms regarding young people's attitudes and behaviour in those settings, and/or ensuring that staff would respond promptly and appropriately if and when risk or harm emerged (Beatriz et al, 2018; Lloyd, 2019). For example, a school-based adolescent dating abuse prevention programme in the US (Safe Dates), which involves a ten-session curriculum, a play performed by students and a poster contest based on curriculum content, has been found not only to reduce adolescent dating abuse in a number of studies across the US, but also to reduce youth weapon carrying in one study, offering promise for modifying a wide range of youth violence manifestations (Foshee et al, 2014). Also in the US, De Pedro et al (2018) found that staff and other pupils were more likely to actively challenge instances of peer victimisation of lesbian, gay, bisexual, transgender and questioning (LGBTQ) young people when: issues regarding sexual orientation and gender identity were covered well within the curriculum and wider discussions in the school; the school actively promoted support groups for students who identified as LGBTQ; and there were anti-bullying policies in place.

A number of studies recommended that safer environments could be built for young people by harnessing the protective capacity of resources offered within their usual communities and spaces, and through the learning and support that peer relationships offered (Murray et al, 2016). There is wide evidence from a range of countries regarding the benefits of bystander intervention programmes, which train students to recognise and challenge situations, behaviours and norms that may lead to violence, and to intervene to prevent a situation from escalating into violence (Letourneau et al, 2017). A randomised controlled trial conducted in 26 US high schools over five years found that the Green Dot bystander intervention programme reduced sexual violence and related forms of interpersonal violence and victimisation in schools (Coker et al, 2017). On a smaller scale, a study of a ten-session mixed-gender psychoeducational group intervention at an urban drop-in centre with 23 runaway, homeless and street youth in the US offered promise for enabling vulnerable young people to learn together to recognise and develop protective factors against domestic minor sex trafficking (Countryman-Roswurm and Bolin, 2014).

To a lesser extent, the review identified social care responses that created community contexts in which young people and their parents could seek safety and support. Reflecting this approach, the Second Chance programme brought together faith-based community and social work organisations in the US, with the aim of reducing domestic minor sex trafficking (Perdue et al, 2012). In addition to the more regular professional support and advocacy provided for individual young people affected by trafficking, this programme set up a coalition of social service and health agencies, law enforcement, faith-based organisations, and interested community members, with the aim of increasing community awareness on human trafficking and developing shared policies and responses. The programme also engaged more broadly with the Federal Bureau of Investigation and policymakers in its efforts to effect legislative change.

A number of authors noted how contextual and structural drivers of EFRH may intersect and reinforce each other, and advised that interventions should be designed with this in mind. Rogers et al (2019) identified the value of working to surface and challenge social norms about domestic violence and abuse in a pilot prevention programme to address problematic peer behaviours and relationships (Change Up), with 13- to 14-year-old students in two UK schools. While the programme was successful in changing young people's perceptions and assumptions in this instance, the study also flagged the importance of education about appropriate relationships and gender equality in schools in view of wider social norms that appear to sanction interpersonal violence or relationship abuse given certain conditions.

Some intervention programmes struggled to achieve their aims when they failed to engage with school, community or peer influences, or did not sufficiently address the additional vulnerabilities of certain groups (Lloyd, 2019). A study of a promising after-school programme (Stand Up Help Out), which was designed to build strengths and reduce peer violence among 'poverty-level' African American youth, yet ignored the reality of their 'high-risk' environments and social disadvantages, produced 'cognitive dissonance' for these young people, who were being encouraged to pursue non-coercive ways of handling interpersonal conflict in peer and romantic relationships amid being continuously exposed to violence in their communities (Bulanda and McCrea, 2013).

A number of papers in the UK noted that while education as a system or process offers opportunities to potentially create safer contexts and relationships for young people, and to enhance their resilience and resources, there is also a concerning relationship between school exclusion/expulsion and young people's exposure to EFRH that may be produced through particular school policies, structures or other features of education systems (All Party Parliamentary Group, 2019; Ofsted, 2019). A national review by the Child Safeguarding Practice Review Panel (2020), focusing on 21 children who either died or had been seriously harmed where criminal exploitation was a factor, noted that 17 of these children had been permanently excluded from mainstream education:

> permanent exclusion was identified by practitioners and family members as a trigger for a significant escalation of risk. Exclusion has a major impact on children's lives and if it is unavoidable then there needs to be immediate wrap-around support to compensate for the lack of structure, sense of belonging and rejection that exclusion from mainstream school can cause. (Child Safeguarding Practice Review Panel, 2020: 8)

Struggling to address structural drivers

The ability of some interventions to meet their desired objectives was reduced or curtailed if services or practitioners failed to consider, or were unable to address, the influence that macrostructural factors, such as poverty and unemployment, had on young people's exposure to EFRH. Challenging social contexts, including high levels of poverty, widespread unemployment, peer networks that focus on alcohol and drug use, and a 'dominant youth masculinity' emphasising toughness and emotional control, limited young males' capacity to benefit from intimate partner violence intervention programmes in South Africa (Gibbs, A., et al, 2015: 220). Also in South Africa, Matthews et al's (2018) evaluation of a multi-component, school-based HIV prevention programme, with a specific focus on decreasing intimate partner violence, revealed that the intervention had a limited impact in reducing sexual risk behaviours among its adolescent recipients. The authors suggest that this might have been because various social and environmental factors that undermine adolescent sexual and reproductive health – such as safe home environments, secure livelihoods and social protection – were not addressed in the programme. Stubbs and Durcan's (2017) evaluation of a well-being intervention in the UK, with the long-term aim of reducing marginalisation and offending, identified how a lack of structural change and persisting contexts of violence compromised the long-term potential impact of the intervention on young people's lives. Once the intervention ended, young people continued to live in a community context in which they were exposed to violence and unable to access employment and mental health support to mitigate the impacts of this exposure.

Other responses to EFRH appeared to target ideas about the harm itself, or prioritise this as the main issue of concern, and, in the process, failed to meet young people's basic needs – needs that underpinned, drove or entrenched their exposure to EFRH. For example, the benefits of an evidence-based intervention (STRIVE) that sought to support homeless young people at risk of sexual exploitation by focusing on family re-engagement were undermined by the failure to respond to young people's essential survival needs or insufficiently enhance their future life opportunities:

> We would be remiss to ignore the social and economic context of risks associated with homelessness and sexual exploitation in our prevention efforts. ... A clinician should be prepared with resources and referrals that not only include ways youth can get their basic needs met but also how to navigate services and systems that help them secure jobs and ultimately survive. (Bounds et al, 2020: 9)

Attending to these challenges, literature on both practice interventions and organisational responses recommended investment in approaches that could address, or at least mitigate, the structural drivers of EFRH (Perdue et al, 2012; Gibbs,

A., et al, 2015; Stubbs and Durcan, 2017; Big Lottery Fund, 2018; Wroe and Lloyd, 2020). Barker et al's (2015) Canadian study of 1,019 'street-involved' youth, for example, noted the barriers these socially and economically vulnerable young people experienced in accessing services. Research focused on either identifying the root causes of EFRH or meeting young people's basic needs often advised interventions that address prior victimisation (and its impact), along with unemployment, the availability of safe community spaces and the impact of both poverty and structural racism on young people's lives (McNeish and Scott, 2018; Astrup, 2019; Public Health England, 2020). A review on knife-crime interventions in the UK, for instance, noted the success of interventions that address young people's concerns about personal safety and perceived vulnerability to victimisation, arguing that 'educational interventions should form part of a sustained effort to reassure young people, and adults, that their fears are taken seriously, and efforts are being made to ensure their safety … the main causes of knife carrying, and the features of any education based initiative should be married up' (Foster, 2013: 10).

In a similar vein, another review, which explored promising practice from the community and voluntary sector on preventing serious youth violence in the UK, underlined the value of a 'whole-system approach', whereby statutory services and voluntary and community organisations partner to develop sustained responses that tackle the root causes of violence (Big Lottery Fund, 2018). Practice flagged as promising in the review included: employing peer mentors with lived experiences; group work; supporting young people to run their own projects or develop business ideas; and extending support to community spaces where young people spend time and feel safe.

Multiple calls for (re)investment in youth service provision were associated with the foregoing. These were particularly trenchant within the UK literature (Association of Directors of Children's Services, 2019; National Youth Agency, 2020), following the 70 per cent reduction in spending on youth services in England and Wales over the past decade (Weale, 2020), but recognition of the role that youth work could play in mitigating the impact of structural inequalities was not reserved to the UK. Barker et al's (2015) study of supports to street-involved youth in Canada, for example, cited the importance of open-access, low-threshold services that were peer driven and youth centric.

The limitations of individualised approaches

In nine papers, authors foregrounded the individualised nature of interventions when explaining the challenges posed by persisting contextual and structural drivers of EFRH. In a review of interventions to address harmful sexual behaviours in adolescence, Letourneau et al (2017) commented on how the historical focus of CSE prevention programmes in schools had been to build the resilience/awareness of young people who might become victims of abuse – as opposed to intervening with the situations/contexts in which such abuse might occur or the young people who might harm others in those situations. The results of their review led the authors to conclude that peer sexual abuse was best responded to via a whole-school approach to harm reduction, as limiting responses to individualised interventions, particularly those that targeted young people who had/might be abused, would likely fail to prevent the abuse of others in the future. This view was further emphasised by Foshee et al (2014), who criticised the way in which siloed and individualised methods of intervention continued to be commissioned, while the results of randomised controlled trials in the US suggested contextual approaches were more effective in addressing various forms of peer abuse in schools, including serious physical violence between peers. Similarly, Lloyd's (2018, 2019) work in the UK highlights the need for responses and interventions regarding harmful sexual behaviours in schools to move beyond responding to individual behaviours and towards creating safer environments within the schools themselves.

The first author of this book has led the development in the UK of the Contextual Safeguarding approach, developed in response to Firmin and colleagues' (2016) recognition that statutory social care systems in England are overwhelmingly designed to target only the children and families affected by EFRH, rather than additionally intervening in the contexts in which EFRH occurs or addressing the structural drivers that underpin it. Such individualised systems are likely to reinforce or even create the conditions in which harm persists (Lloyd and Firmin, 2020; Wroe and Lloyd, 2020; Wroe, 2021). A Contextual Safeguarding approach is underpinned by four domains, stipulating that for child protection systems to adequately address EFRH, they should: (1) design services that target the contexts of harm; (2) incorporate extra-familial contexts into child protection frameworks (rather than crime prevention frameworks); (3) develop partnerships with organisations and services that have a reach into these contexts (beyond the usual statutory partners); and (4) measure outcomes not just through the individual changes to young people's behaviours, but also in relation to changing the contexts where harm occurs (Firmin, 2020). Over the past five years, the contextual safeguarding research programme has supported local authorities, voluntary and community sector organisations, and schools in England and Wales to develop or redesign their safeguarding systems, with the aim of enabling them to better identify and respond to EFRH. While the approach has demonstrated its efficacy in system design, evidence of enhanced safety outcomes for young people has not yet been established and further testing is necessary (Lefevre et al, 2020).

Conclusion: the need for system change

The review surfaced complexity in respect of the evidence base for responding to contextual and structural drivers of EFRH.

For the most part, it is studies of practice interventions, rather than of system/organisational responses, that have evidenced the value of creating safety in contexts, as well as for individuals. The evidence base for this appears to be strong – particularly in creating safe peer and school contexts associated with various forms of peer-instigated EFRH. However, publications on both interventions and systems noted a persistent commitment to individualised practices; therefore, much of the evidence featured in this chapter emerged from critiques of approaches that failed to address contextual factors or evaluations that found structural barriers to sustaining the impact of otherwise effective responses. As such, the literature flags the absence of contextual interventions as an underlying limitation and highlights the need for systems in which to hold and sustain such interventions.

Moreover, it cautions against viewing responses abstracted from wider structural factors that are highly relevant to young people's exposure to EFRH. Yet, the review was unable to surface evidence of systems or interventions that successfully addressed both contextual and structural drivers of EFRH in a sustained and consistent manner, suggesting the need for system change (at least in the UK) for this to be feasible.

SIX

Addressing the specific dynamics of risk and harm

Introduction

By definition, 'extra-familial' risks and harms occur beyond young people's homes and caretaking relationships, and there is increasing recognition regarding the difficulties that parents and carers experience in supporting, guiding and protecting their adolescent children with respect to unsafe situations and associations of which they have limited awareness or control over (Thomas and D'Arcy, 2017; Pike et al, 2019). Our review indicated that this extra-familial element created specific dynamics that required services to reconsider the way they designed and delivered interventions. However, shortcomings in the current provision remain, posing challenges to those tasked with improving practices for young people affected by EFRH.

To some extent, this is not surprising. The primary role of social care over recent decades – particularly in the UK, US and Australia – has been to provide family support and address safeguarding concerns where the caregiving is deemed inadequate or abusive (Featherstone et al, 2018). While most of the practice interventions featured in this review were developed with specific forms of EFRH in mind, many are delivered within wider child welfare or safeguarding systems that have largely been designed around the *family* as the locus for intervention and that struggle to accommodate the specific dynamics of EFRH. As such, one third of the literature we reviewed covering organisational responses and one fifth of the literature on practice interventions recommended that future services and systems should be designed with EFRH in mind. Just under half of these documents made recommendations related to legislation or policy design at a national level, and a smaller group recommended the redesign of statutory social care systems at a local level to improve responses.

Across these recommendations, three themes emerged. First, social care systems and services currently centring around familial (largely parenting) assessment and intervention need to broaden their scope to include peer, school and community contexts where EFRH occurs. Second, responses to EFRH need to be welfare, rather than criminal justice, oriented, including for young people whose experiences might involve both victimisation and perpetration, or who have committed other offences in the context of being victimised through EFRH. Finally, services need to recognise and respond to the gains (material and otherwise) that young people may experience when caught up in EFRH. In this chapter, we explore what each of these recommendations suggest about the dynamics of EFRH and the implications for the design of future social care responses.

Responding beyond parenting or family-focused intervention

Literature from the UK (Hanson and Holmes, 2014; Institute of Public Care, 2015; Luke, 2017; Pike et al, 2019), US (Fong and Cardoso, 2010; Liles et al, 2016; McGuire, 2018) and Australia (Firmin and Rayment-McHugh, 2020) has questioned the narrow focus of conventional social care and child welfare systems that target families (and particularly the parenting role) for intervention and are not optimised for addressing EFRH. Broadening the scope of social care responses beyond parenting interventions appeared to be a particular challenge for statutory (as opposed to voluntary) social care organisations and systems. Within such systems, parents may be responsibilised for their child's vulnerability to risk, for example, rather than being valued and supported as resourceful collaborators: 'Parents felt strongly that the predominant attitude of Children's Social Care towards parents of children being sexually exploited was fundamentally wrong. Their experience was of social care staff being fixated on parents as the problem rather than seeing them as partners in safeguarding' (Pike et al, 2019: 32). Some authors recommended moving away from individualised social work case management systems. Stanley and Guru (2015), for example, argued that in the case of radicalisation, locating risk and interventions solely in individual children or family members can obscure associated underlying social and political factors, and further alienate families through creating a relationship of surveillance, rather than one of trust.

In response to this too-narrow focus, a range of UK publications recommended that social care systems be redesigned to better engage with the groups, spaces and other contexts beyond the home where EFRH is known to occur (see, for example, Home Affairs Select Committee, 2019; Wroe, 2021; Lloyd and Firmin, 2020). This recommendation was supported by an international set of papers (discussed in detail in Chapter Five) that recommended interventions into peer-group relationships and norms (Bulanda and McCrea, 2013; Countryman-Roswurm and Bolin, 2014; McLeod et al, 2015; Coker et al, 2017; De Pedro et al, 2018; Rogers et al, 2019), as well as other age-specific contexts that informed the nature of EFRH, such as community (Pritchard and Svistak, 2014; McNeish and Scott, 2018), school (Petering et al, 2014; Murray et al, 2016) and sports (Miller et al, 2013) settings.

In Australia, for example, academics at Griffiths University partnered with organisations in Aboriginal and Torres Strait

Islander communities to develop responses to peer-to-peer sexual abuse that responded holistically to the social contexts in which this harm was occurring (Firmin and Rayment-McHugh 2020). Interventions comprised: a training programme for teachers at a local Indigenous school to build guardianship capacity and develop whole-school responses to peer-to-peer sexual abuse; an environmental assessment of school buildings and grounds; and increased police guardianship in the local area. These activities were complementary to a parenting programme specifically tailored to parents in this community and clinical programmes that targeted individual young people, alongside a range of prevention activities targeting other community settings, including both public spaces and home environments. Noteworthily, this work sat outside of, rather than forming part of, social care systems in that part of Australia (Firmin and Rayment-McHugh, 2020).

Several UK studies have also demonstrated the usefulness of interventions formed outside of the statutory system, including through social workers forming partnerships with organisations who are more expert in working with adolescents and/or in contexts beyond families to enhance their reach and understanding in response to EFRH (Pearce, 2014). Thomas and D'Arcy (2017) described how the voluntary sector may be harnessed both to 'build bridges' between parents/carers and statutory services when developing protective factors against CSE within family and/or foster homes, and to partner with social care teams and community groups to raise awareness of exploitation across the wider community.

Rebalancing towards welfare-oriented system responses

A number of sources suggested that there was a need to rebalance social care systems and interventions in favour of welfare and public-health orientations where they were currently solely or principally organised around criminal justice aims and procedures. Goldenberg et al (2013) have discussed how current approaches to preventing sex trafficking in Mexico, for example, tend to criminalise girls and young women, rather than address the contextual factors connected with their exploitation, such as homelessness and poverty. The authors advocate for interventions that boost young women's social supports, public-health prevention programmes that are trauma informed and peer-based education and other economic alternatives that offer routes out of commercial sexual exploitation. Other papers highlight the criminalisation of young people affected by EFRH in the UK and the disproportionate nature with which Black young people, and Black young males specifically, are monitored and sanctioned, rather than protected. Williams (2018) draws particular attention to criticisms of the Gangs Violence Matrix, introduced in the UK in 2012, which consists of a database listing people suspected of being associated with 'gang'-related criminal activity and employs a set of algorithms to generate a 'violence ranking' for individuals – a ranking widely deplored for its racial disparity. Some literature suggests that the term 'gang' is a historically and inherently racialised term that increases young people's chances of criminalisation (see, for example, Williams and Clarke, 2016), often on little evidence, and that alienates and stereotypes young people. The underlying culture of surveillance towards young people suspected of being connected to crime, as reflected in the increased practice of stop and search in the UK, Williams (2018) further argues, indicates a lack of awareness from police officers about their statutory obligation to safeguard the welfare of children. Challenges like these speak to the potential risks and limitations of interagency approaches set out in Chapter Four: increased information sharing could actually exacerbate the structural harms noted in Chapter Five, rather than address the sources of EFRH that young people face.

The issues surfaced by Goldenberg et al (2013) and Williams (2018) also emerged in other papers featured in the review. A need for both practice systems and interventions to accommodate a blurring of 'victim' and 'perpetrator' identities was noted in studies from Canada (Barker et al, 2015), the US (Sapiro et al, 2016; McGuire, 2018) and the UK (Hudek, 2018a, 2018b; Turner et al, 2019). As a round-table discussion of politicians and experts in the UK, which reviewed the needs of, and service responses to, children who go missing and are criminally exploited by 'gangs', noted:

> Worryingly, vulnerable children and young people who are trafficked and exploited by gangs to distribute drugs are still too often perceived to have 'made a choice' and are therefore criminalised rather than safeguarded and recognised as victims of the gangs who control them. ... It is important that professionals start seeing young people who are involved in gangs as potential victims of exploitation or trafficking and that all young people under 18 are considered children, are treated as such, and are safeguarded by society. (All-Party Parliamentary Group for Runaway and Missing Children and Adults, 2017: 2)

Relatedly, McGuire (2018), with reference to victims of trafficking in the US, argued that arresting and detaining adolescent victims of trafficking, even where this protects them, results in re-traumatisation. As was noted in Chapter Three, such enforced interventions can further erode young people's trust in professionals and, by causing them to withdraw their engagement, may place them at additional risk.

However, the recommendation that professionals should engage more productively with the overlaps in victimisation and perpetration that are often a feature of young people drawn into EFRH requires further attention in two respects. First, in the UK at least, it appears more challenging for social care systems and professionals to straddle the polarisations that tend to arise for forms of EFRH that occur via criminality and with or by peers. A solution for the former has been to remove the criminalisation of behaviours associated with particular forms of EFRH. For example, in countries like the UK and US, legislation has been amended so that young people (under the age of 18) cannot be charged with offences related to 'prostitution'. Redesignating these situations as CSE (the UK) or domestic minor sex trafficking (the US) dismantles an initial barrier to integrative responses, as the harm itself is no longer criminalised. This approach does not resolve any other offences that young people may commit in the context of their abuse – such as criminal damage of the children's home they are living in, theft of alcohol as a means of managing post-traumatic stress responses or the recruitment of other young people into exploitative networks to reduce their own exposure to abuse. However, it does create a policy context that is more conducive with recognising the victimisation of young people abused in extra-familial contexts and relationships.

There is no equivalent policy development for other forms of EFRH – particularly those occurring via criminality and/ or peers. Where young people are criminally exploited to hold, sell or transport illegal substances, and, in the process of this, required to carry weapons or inflict violence on others, they commit a range of offences. These young people are then identified as perpetrators of crime, with social care services struggling to offer a welfare-based response (Hudek, 2018a, 2018b; Turner et al, 2019). Similarly, with peer-related violence and abuse, young people come to the attention of services and professionals as both having *been harmed* and having *harmed others*. Sources in the review found that young people displaying harmful sexual behaviours within wider contexts of peer violence were often responded to via criminal justice, rather than child welfare, agencies (Clements et al, 2017; Firmin et al, 2019). This reduced the ability of wider systems to attend to the experiences of victimisation that often underpinned or were associated with their offending behaviours.

The second feature of the victim–perpetrator overlap that warranted more detailed consideration came from contributions by authors such as Barker et al (2015), Williams (2018) and

Wroe (2021), whose work reminds us that this tension is best viewed through an intersectional lens. Not all young people affected by EFRH will experience this tension in the same way. As young people get older, the ability of services to see them as victims, as well as perpetrators, of harms diminishes. Considering how responses engage with 'age', particularly in the latter part of adolescence, is therefore relevant to how this challenge is resolved. Likewise, Williams' caution around the racialised response to 'gangs' and serious youth violence in England – and the implications for Black young people being over-policed and under-protected – suggests that, again, services may struggle to see the vulnerability and victim experiences of Black young people to the extent that they do for their white peers. The under-identification of young men who are sexually exploited, as compared with young women, has also been a point of contention for over a decade (Leon and Raws, 2016; Josenhans et al, 2020).

EFRH therefore requires that social care responses work with adolescents who straddle victim–perpetrator identities. Creating 'victim' services or 'perpetrator' programmes that assume clear water between these two identities will likely fall short for a number of adolescents affected by these issues – particularly as young people themselves often do not self-identify or even understand such labels. Yet, in many countries featured in this review, the policy framework from which services offer their response maintains a victim–perpetrator divide and continues to risk criminalising young people who commit offences in the context of their abuse, particularly as they transition from children's to adults' services (over the age of majority).

Recognising and responding to the 'gains' of EFRH

The practice tensions of working with victim–perpetrator overlaps seem exacerbated in situations where young people apparently benefit, in some way, in the context of being harmed. During the review, this issue was particularly pronounced for EFRH that occurs via exploitation – be that sexual or criminal. Research from Australia and from the UK documented various ways in which young people who were being sexually or criminally exploited did not always recognise their own victimisation due to the gain/benefit (material or otherwise) they received in exchange for the harm they experienced (Reisel, 2017; McKibbin and Humphreys, 2019; Robinson et al, 2019). This failure to recognise young people's exploitation may be mirrored by social care professionals who perceive young people to be making agentic choices about their involvement in EFRH (Sapiro et al, 2016). Likewise, Robinson et al (2019) highlight the need for professionals to recognise that adolescents who are victims of criminal exploitation through the supply or selling of drugs challenge neat victim–perpetrator demarcations. The idea of 'gain', like 'perpetration', appears to taint the victim identity of young people affected by EFRH and therefore impact the ability of social care organisations to respond effectively and holistically. This seems particularly so within systems/organisations designed with an 'innocent child victim' in mind.

Attending to these challenges, 16 papers (almost exclusively drawn from UK contexts) recommended that legal frameworks be reoriented to a welfare, as opposed to criminal justice, approach to EFRH. Calls were made to improve protections for young people who were criminally exploited – in particular, how to manage their involvement in serious offences and financial gain as a result of grooming or coercion, and how to safeguard them from the very real threat of retributions should they be seen to desist or share information on their exploiters (Hudek, 2018a, 2018b; Robinson et al, 2019; Turner et al, 2019). As a national review of social care responses to criminal exploitation in England in 2020 concluded: a better understanding was required of trends and patterns associated with criminal exploitation; a new practice framework was needed that was tailored to the particular nature of this form of exploitation; and the ability of the current statutory process (National Referral Mechanism) to protect adolescents from prosecution should be reviewed (Child Safeguarding Practice Review Panel, 2020). Likewise, in the US (Stone, 2011) and UK (Lloyd, 2018), authors recommended reforming legislation underpinning responses to sexual offences when applied to cases of abuse through sexual image sharing among young people, as 'to categorise all sexual image sharing as illegal but suggest practitioners should not criminalise young people makes responding to the abusive forms of image sharing a challenge' (Lloyd, 2018: 785).

Conclusion: fit for purpose?

Findings from this review suggest that child welfare and social care systems in the UK require adaptation to sufficiently engage with the dynamics of EFRH. The challenges that led to this recommendation are also evidenced in other countries featured in this review. While practice interventions discussed in the literature were specifically designed for situations of EFRH involving adolescents, the wider systems within which such interventions are offered generally were not. Most of the systems described in the literature (particularly statutory systems) had been designed to address parenting difficulties or safeguarding concerns, often with reference to younger children, and interventions were largely targeted through family-based approaches. What young people caught up in EFRH appear to require, by contrast, are social care systems that can reach beyond family homes and relationships to generate and sustain protective mechanisms, and that can provide a sufficiently nuanced response for young people whose victimisation coincides with offending or results in some form of material or social gain. Without the ability to work in these flexible and porous ways, responses to EFRH may be driven by criminal justice concerns, rather than oriented towards child welfare aspirations, particularly for young men, racially minoritised young people and those who are ageing out of childhood and into adulthood.

Some of these challenges are mitigated, to an extent, by the approaches shared in previous chapters – for example, by developing interventions that work with peer, school and community contexts, or by facilitating shared (and interagency) understandings of EFRH, adolescence and vulnerability. It is not clear, however, whether such approaches will alone resolve the limitations surfaced in this chapter.

SEVEN

A youth-centred paradigm

Introduction

In Western contexts, the relationship between children and their caregivers commonly begins to shift during the years of adolescence, as young people spend increasing amounts of time socialising away from parental supervision and become heavily influenced by peer relationships (Sawyer et al, 2018). Developmentally, adolescence is also associated with a drive towards independence and 'increased risk-taking, impulsivity, sensation-seeking and sexual interest' (Hanson and Holmes, 2014: 9). Perhaps unsurprisingly, then, young people's exposure to EFRH rises during the teenage years (Sidebotham et al, 2016; Her Majesty's Government, 2018; Pona and Turner, 2018: Brandon et al, 2020; NSPCC, 2020). Many practice interventions and some organisational responses to EFRH are designed around such dynamics of adolescent development to maximise young people's engagement with services and build safety.

Three features characterise the development of youth-centred systems and interventions. First, they are collaborative in seeking to offer (or create) opportunities for young people to exercise agency and choice. Second, they are designed with particular identity features in mind, such as age, gender or ethnicity (and the intersections of these). Finally, of particular significance, they can not only recognise the trauma caused by EFRH and its impact on a young person's behaviour, but also assist a young person to recover or cope given the trauma they have experienced. In this chapter, we detail each of these features and their implications for future social care responses to EFRH. We also note that many of these youth-centred characteristics of practice systems and models additionally focus on addressing the dynamics of EFRH described in Chapter Five and harness some of the relationships that were detailed in Chapter Three.

Collaborative and choice-focused support

During adolescence, young people display an increasing desire for autonomy. As such, they will make choices (sometimes in constrained circumstances) about engaging, or not, with interventions and support offered to them. In recognition of this, various publications that we reviewed described the ways in which practice models and systems create service offers that respect young people's choice and agency, and support collaborative practices. These approaches, in turn, increase the chances of sustained engagement, which bolsters routes to protection.

Papers on practice interventions, and, to a lesser extent, organisational responses, emphasised approaches that build a young person's capacity to cope in, or exit from, situations of EFRH. These include offering tools for anger management and conflict resolution, and enabling young people to develop skills that would enhance their employability and provide routes to economic independence away from exploitation (Foshee et al, 2014; Gibbs, A., et al, 2015). A programme for pregnant African American adolescent girls, for instance, was designed to support skills and learning about healthy and non-violent relationships, communication and conflict management, emotional regulation, coping, stress, and time management.

Positive impacts were noted, not only on participants' own behaviours in partner relationships, but also through reductions in their experiences of intimate partner violence (IPV) victimisation (Langhinrichsen-Rohling and Turner, 2012).

Young people can be empowered towards self-protection through information and education about the supports and assistance they could access in situations of EFRH, should they wish to do so (Black et al, 2012). Where young people are offered services that require them to actively opt in, they are found to experience some measure of beneficial control over their involvement with professionals (Coy, 2017). Some responses focused on providing a safe space that young people can access when in need, as with the programmes for young people experiencing CSE/domestic minor sex trafficking evaluated by D.A. Gibbs et al (2015). All of these responses adopt a consent-based approach to support: ensuring that young people know where to access help, but relying on them to follow that through.

One way to increase the likelihood of such follow-through is to ensure services can meet young people's basic needs, rather than solely focusing on the EFRH. Some papers emphasised the importance of addressing issues that may be contributing to, be a consequence of or run in parallel with EFRH (Coy, 2017; Hardy et al, 2013). As an example of housing as a contributing factor, if young people are not in safe accommodation, they may be exploited by others in exchange for somewhere to stay. The trauma a young person may experience as a result of EFRH may lead to stress responses that involve challenging behaviour and increase conflict in their home environment, and family relationships can break down; access to a lack of safe accommodation in this situation would then be a consequence of EFRH (Fong and Cardoso, 2010; Barker et al, 2015). Alternatively, contributing and consequential factors may run in parallel to each other; however, professionals may focus on EFRH and neglect other needs, such as housing. According to Hardy et al (2013: 14):

a focus on such aspects as basic living skills and decision making, physical and biological health management, and educational and career decision making are important for assessment and intervention. ... The need for food, clothing, and shelter are three of the primary barriers to victims leaving their circumstances ... [and shelters] should provide a haven for the individual to transition from the traumatic experience to reintegration into society.

Young people's engagement with services was further facilitated by offering flexibility and choice around the length and nature of support that young people could access. Both the dynamic nature of EFRH and the changes that come with adolescent development require services to be responsive and work with a young person at their pace, rather than to a standardised model of support (Gibbs, D.A., et al, 2015). This was seen with a UK project supporting girls and young women who had experienced CSE and violence, which flexed from an initially fixed six-month period of engagement to an approach that was better tailored to individual needs and responded iteratively to complexities in the young women's lives (Coy, 2017). As discussed in Chapter Three, several papers recognised that some EFRH interventions can, or should, be short-term (Langhinrichsen-Rohling and Turner, 2012; Gibbs, D.A., et al, 2015). In their review of 17 interventions to address youth-perpetrated physical or sexual violence, varying in length from three months through to two years, Fagan and Catalano (2013) found that even short and intensive approaches could have a significant and lasting impact on violence reduction. This was particularly the case for intensive therapeutic programmes and for interventions embedded in school curricula or parenting programmes. Like interventions that educate young people on where they can access support, these approaches either meet young people's specific needs at any given time or create connections to forms of support that they can access (and that will be sustained) beyond the lifetime of a professional intervention.

Examples were given of how more flexible, choice-oriented, youth-centred practice systems and interventions could result when these were co-produced with young people, who were seen as experts in their own lives. Stubbs and Durcan (2017: 6) outlined how a community-based holistic well-being and mental health service in England (Project Future) was co-designed with young men aged 16–25 with experiences of the criminal justice system, particularly those exposed to serious youth violence or labelled 'gang affiliated'. Recognising the role that inequalities and marginalisation play in EFRH, the project was successful in enhancing these young men's access to education, employment and training opportunities, as well as to services offering support with housing, benefits and mental and physical health needs. The project was underpinned by efforts to create an environment of safety, respect, acceptance, empowerment and legitimacy, echoed by the systemic approach described by Van de Vijver and Harvey (2019). The latter found that giving young people safe spaces to explore their experiences – without immediate challenge, labelling or imposition of interpretations by professionals – enabled them to engage with supports and interventions in a more meaningful way. This involved building up relationships of trust and maintaining positions of 'safe uncertainty', which 'allows the practitioner to remain curious and responsive while also being sure there is safety in the relationship and work being undertaken' (Van de Vijver and Harvey, 2019: 456).

Finally, a number of papers emphasised the need for EFRH-related services and interventions to create the necessary conditions within which young people could exercise choice and influence the direction of their own interventions. This approach was exemplified through Van de Vijver and Harvey's fictional composite vignette of their systemically oriented work with young women at risk of CSE in the UK:

When trying to support young people to move away from the danger of the grooming pattern, it is tempting to think that by explaining the process and risks, the young person will be able to disentangle themselves. As professionals within children's services, it can feel compelling to say to the young person that they are being coerced or forced into actions and that they are putting themselves in risky and unsafe situations. ... However, we found again and again that by positioning ourselves in this way, this seemed to position the young people in feeling they had to defend their own and other's actions. This resulted in a stalemate and without any improvements in safety. It also showed the young people that we did not understand their experience, as we were not entering into the logic of the world they were living in. Instead, what has helped in our relationship with Zara has been not challenging the logic or meaning of her actions, but giving her space to explore her experiences herself. (Van de Vijver and Harvey, 2019: 457–8)

These more collaborative, youth-centred approaches require the creation of safeguarding systems that work with young people – and their parents – as partners in safety planning (Eaton and Holmes, 2017; Pike et al, 2019). This position is reinforced by papers that call for policymakers to resolve the tension, apparent in practices in multiple countries, of how to acknowledge the agency of young people who have also been victimised (Firmin et al, 2016; Sapiro et al, 2016; Reisel, 2017; McGuire, 2018; Lefevre et al, 2019). McKibbin and Humphreys (2019) found fundamental differences between the ways in which Australian residential care workers and young people themselves constructed vulnerability, agency and consent in the context of CSE and harmful sexual behaviours: the professionals considered young people primarily to be vulnerable victims of exploitation, who required guidance and protection, and were concerned that many young people were rejecting the 'victim' label. The authors suggest that collaborative approaches that do not frame victimisation and agency as mutually exclusive, and instead recognise and work with young people's ability to make good decisions for themselves, are likely to be more successful in preventing exploitation. This echoes Sapiro et al's (2016: 108) findings in the US that services for young people need to recognise 'the complex balance of agency and vulnerability … [and] find ways to protect adolescents who have been subject to abuse, while respecting and supporting their growing agency'.

Intersecting identities, needs and experiences

While extensive, the ability of interventions and systems to offer choice was not the only way that youth-focused responses were evidenced in the review. The ways in which services engaged (or not) with young people's varying and intersecting identities were also a point of discussion. A range of equalities issues were raised as being relevant to how interventions were designed and delivered.

Bringing together reflections on flexible working, participatory approaches and the need for age-appropriate support, Barker et al (2015) called for open-access youth service provision in Canada, based on peer referrals, to be available to young people as they transition into adult services:

> Among our sample, each additional year of age was statistically associated with a greater likelihood of reporting difficulty in accessing services. In this study setting, youth services typically terminate between the ages of 21 and 24 years, compelling young adults to turn to adult services that may be problematic and present dangers. … The establishment of a continuum of services with gradual age transitions for street-involved youth could improve service access for those who now 'age-out' of youth services and find adult services inappropriate or suboptimal. (Barker et al, 2015: 357)

Problems associated with safeguarding young people as they move towards legal adulthood have been highlighted through the emergence of the concept of 'transitional safeguarding' in the UK. This emphasises the need for systems and services to become more attuned to the developmental needs and life experiences of young people as they approach the age of majority, and for adults' services to recognise that vulnerabilities and protection needs in respect of EFRH matter beyond childhood (Holmes and Smale, 2018). Co-design, participative approaches, peer referrals and the involvement of trained peer supporters in services have all been found to be valuable in working with young people ageing into adult-focused services. For example, Sturrock (2012) describes a UK project (Catch 22) that employed trained peer advisors, while also offering young adults the opportunity to gain a qualification in providing information, advice and guidance. Likewise, in their study of a community-based response to CSE/domestic minor sex trafficking in the US, Perdue et al (2012) show how supporting survivors into adulthood through a programme involving peer supporters and peer-led groups, alongside professional social work facilitation, enabled young people to transition from victims at first, to survivors and, eventually, to becoming 'thrivers' in relation to personal, social, economic and spiritual development.

Some papers emphasised the importance of interventions being age appropriate in relation to considering young people's social and cognitive developmental stage, as the contexts or relationships that can be effectively targeted when young people are aged 11 may differ for 15- or 19-year-olds (Petering et al, 2014; Pritchard and Svistak, 2014; Murray et al, 2016). For example, in their study reviewing a range of youth violence prevention programmes in the US, Fagan and Catalano (2013: 142) advocate for 'delivering services during every stage of development and for youth from all backgrounds and levels of risk' as a way of enabling communities to reduce problems of youth violence, with particular attention given to peer and community processes.

Focused attention has been given to how gendered patterns in the nature of EFRH and its impact on young people should be considered in the design or delivery of services, particularly with reference to group-based interventions. Kernsmith and Hernandez-Jozefowicz (2011) reported how the gender-sensitive approach of a peer-education sexual assault prevention programme in the US, emphasising male responsibility for decreasing rape within mixed-gender groups, led to significant changes in attitudes among both male and female students. Other studies evidenced variations in how young women and young men engaged in or benefited from peer-based interventions. Black et al's (2012) study of youth-dating violence and sexual assault prevention programmes in US schools found that boys benefited most from participation in same-gender work and girls from mixed-gender work. However, this differed in respect of interventions reported for young people more directly involved in or at risk from EFRH. Berry et al (2017), for example, noted that gender-specific groups for young women who had experienced CSE in the UK promoted participants' feelings of safety, particularly since most of them had experienced male perpetration. The Safe Choices project in the UK, aiming to address sexual exploitation and violence affecting girls and young women in the context of 'gang' association, layered a feminist analysis into its group and individual interventions:

> There were two elements to the feminist ethos of the project, both valued by young women: the gender-informed analysis of sexual exploitation and violence that connects social and sexualised sexism to young women's lives; and a feminist relational approach to women supporting women ... valuing active participation; connecting private 'troubles' with public 'issues'; and promoting relationships with workers and other young women. (Coy, 2017: 17–18)

Knowledge about the particular vulnerabilities of LGBT+ young people in relation to EFRH is still formative (Scott et al, 2017a; Public Health England, 2020), and this needs to be improved if services are to be tailored appropriately to the needs, characteristics and preferences of this group (De Pedro et al, 2018). More work is also needed to understand the barriers to protection and receiving support for young people with learning disabilities: 'The reasons for this are multi-layered and complex and often appear to be entrenched in the way society perceives and treats young people with learning disabilities. Previous studies on disabled children's abuse point to the part that disablism can play in their lack of protection' (Franklin and Smeaton, 2017: 480).

Finally, although more limited in the publications sourced through this review, there was some consideration of how racism and issues of cultural sensitivity should inform youth-focused service responses to EFRH. As has been noted in earlier chapters, young people from racialised minorities are more likely to be seen as agentic in their involvement in EFRH, to have their victimhood minimised and to receive criminal justice-oriented monitoring and sanctions, which are ineffective in disrupting young people's involvement in violent crime as victims or perpetrators (Williams, 2018). Recommendations are made regarding: effective and non-stigmatising engagement with minoritised communities to enable meaningful co-production in service design; improving early intervention so that it builds young people's resilience; and ensuring practitioners and the interventions they deliver are culturally competent (Hughes et al, 2015; Hudek, 2018a; National Youth Agency, 2020). The need to recognise and address racism and the intersections between racism and class, age and gender have also been noted (Coy, 2017).

Consideration of young people's varied, and intersectional, lived experiences (and therefore needs) appeared to facilitate the collaboration and choice-based approaches documented earlier in this chapter. In many respects, these two elements of service/system design, while discrete features, go hand in hand to ensure the feasibility of each other.

Trauma-informed practices

Finally, the review revealed that the ability of systems and practitioners to recognise the presence of trauma, and, in some instances, take a trauma-informed approach, was an important component in the design of EFRH interventions. Recommendations here stemmed, in part, from a recognition that experiences of EFRH were associated with complex trauma, and hence service design needed to ameliorate the impact of this (McGuire, 2018; Christie, 2018; Hudek, 2018b). The creation of safe, compassionate, supportive spaces within which young people can express feelings of trauma, start to make their own choices and decisions without coercion and manipulation, and begin to trust safe others was emphasised. Muraya and Fry (2016), for example, propose the shaping of aftercare services for victims of child trafficking around principles of rescue, recovery and reintegration. Kohli et al (2015) highlight how young people who have experienced trafficking need professional relationships that offer safety and seek to establish trust, alongside advocacy and help with navigating the complexity of support systems.

Trauma-informed practice also recognises connections between young people's earlier developmental trauma and their subsequent vulnerability to, or involvement in, EFRH (Hickle and Lefevre, 2022). Literature within this review considered how a trauma-informed approach recognises, and works with, such behaviours as 'going missing' as symptoms of harm and/or coping mechanisms in situations of EFRH. By working with young people with this understanding at the forefront, practitioners are able to offer support that speaks to young people's needs and, where possible, counters – rather than reinforces – previous experiences of being misunderstood, blamed and controlled by others (McGuire, 2018; Hardy et al (2013) highlighted how for many survivors of child trafficking and exploitation, extended periods of coercion and mistrust earlier in their lives present barriers to their ability to develop relationships, connection and a sense of belonging. The impact of social stigma and stereotyping, victimhood being misidentified/ignored, and the surveillance and criminalisation of young people's lives intersects with these experiences and further serves to undermine the success of interventions seeking to re-establish connection and a sense of belonging and identity for young people (Williams, 2018).

From 'doing to' to 'working with'

This chapter has detailed how and why youth centredness forms the fifth characteristic in our typology of promising or effective responses to EFRH. To work within a youth-centred paradigm, social care interventions and systems need to: facilitate choice and create spaces for collaboration; engage with young people's varying identities (and associated needs and experiences); and recognise and respond to trauma. In the absence of these characteristics, professional responses run the risk of problematising and controlling (rather than facilitating) young people's choices, punishing young people for displaying symptoms of trauma (albeit as an intended means of protection), and even re-traumatising them in so doing. While having space for collaboration and choice is important, the nature of that collaboration and the types of choices made are likely to vary across ages and depending on lived experiences. Considering young people's intersectional needs is critical here: what is experienced as a youth-centred response by a 12-year-old white girl might be quite different experienced by a 20-year-old Black young man.

Core to all of this, however, is the creation of social care responses that *work with* young people rather than *do to* them. Such approaches are also relevant for developing relational practices and responses that acknowledge the specific dynamics of EFRH, such as the overlaps between victimisation and perpetration. Furthermore, evidence that systems need to create the conditions in which young people can exercise choice speaks to the importance of contextual and structural interventions, as highlighted in Chapter Five of this book. A youth-centred paradigm not only seeks to foster collaboration with young people, but also ensures that such collaboration is safe and sustainable.

EIGHT

A framework for designing and improving responses

Introduction

Over the course of Chapters Three to Seven, we have outlined the five characteristics of promising or effective social care responses to EFRH. Such responses need to be: (1) relational; (2) interagency; (3) contextual; (4) EFRH focused; and (5) youth centred. Each response characteristic offers discrete potential to improve service responses: some organisations may focus on building relationships between professionals and young people to disrupt EFRH, for example; others may redesign services previously intended for younger children to better meet the needs and preferences of young people. Our review surfaced criticisms and challenges of social care responses to EFRH, as well as examples of effectiveness, and we noted that while there may be merit in developing services through the application of these characteristics in isolation, it was at their intersection that they most seemed to flourish. Moreover, it could be seen that the challenges of introducing one characteristic might be overcome when integrated with another; for example, the risks of surveillance of young people involved in criminal activity through enhanced information sharing across agencies (see Chapter Four) may be offset when a service has an awareness of, and ability to engage with, the overlapping victim–perpetrator identities that may occur for young people affected by EFRH (see Chapter Six).

As such, we concluded that the five response characteristics presented in this book would be best implemented in combination. Furthermore, for service improvement and (re)design to be most successful, policy and service landscapes needed to be conducive to their application. Our analysis indicated that this would be facilitated if social care organisations and systems operated the following three system principles:

- employ contextual *and* relational interventions as reinforcing, rather than opposing, practice approaches;
- trouble and re-envision the social work role and definitions of vulnerability; and
- mitigate, and avoid reinforcing, the impact of structural harm on young people's safety and well-being.

In this chapter, we outline the role played by each system principle in deepening how the social care response characteristics are understood and illustrate their interconnectivity. We end by offering a framework for improving or (re)designing future service responses to EFRH.

Using contextual and relational interventions as reinforcing approaches to intervention

Our review evidenced that responses to EFRH need to both build relationships (see Chapter Three) and intervene with contexts associated with harm (see Chapter Five); however, for the most part, these two characteristics were studied (and used in practice) discretely. Publications that evidence or promote safety through relationships tend to focus on responses to EFRH via exploitation or EFRH via sexual harm. They describe approaches that: foster trust between young people and professionals; create space for collaboration between young people, families and professionals; and have the potential to build supportive community networks around young people affected by EFRH. Conversely, publications charting responses to EFRH via peers or EFRH via criminality are more likely to pilot or promote interventions with the school, peer and community contexts where this harm occurs. Such interventions foster positive peer-support networks and influence the social conditions that are conducive to EFRH.

The tendency to silo relational and contextual approaches is well illustrated by publications on responses to young people who display 'harmful sexual behaviours' compared to those affected by 'serious youth violence'. Much of the literature on responses to harmful sexual behaviours evaluated therapeutic interventions with young people (Clements et al, 2017; McNeish and Scott, 2018). The problematic behaviours these young people displayed were framed as associated with their psychological needs. The same cannot be said of literature on serious youth violence, where contextual and wider structural drivers dominate the narrative (Fagan and Catalano, 2013; McNeish and Scott, 2018). For both these forms of EFRH, young people instigate harm against peers, but one cohort is situated as traumatised and the other as impoverished. There are exceptions to this. In the US, Letourneau et al (2017) called for contextual responses to harmful sexual behaviours – a position aligned with studies into contextual responses to peer abuse in schools, including serious youth violence (Foshee et al, 2014). These publications situate contexts associated with adolescent development ahead of all other targets of intervention, but they are in the minority when it comes to literature on EFRH via sexual harm and via exploitation.

The division between how relational and contextual responses to EFRH are presented is reflective of a wider split in social work practice and research: between therapeutic and relational orientations to working with families facing adversity (individual deficit), and the more radical social work end, which emphasises structural disadvantage and oppression, and seeks solutions to address that wider context – and, in so doing, might risk missing the individual experience and therapeutic needs (Payne, 2020).

While we have highlighted that the five response characteristics presented in this book flourish most when considered together, it is relational and contextual responses that most need to be interwoven and reinforcing of each other. Given the increasing desire for autonomy and the emphasis on extra-familial relationships that characterise adolescence, professionals work most effectively when they engage in collaborative, flexible and choice-based relationships with young people. Further, trusted relationships have the potential to build safety in contexts, particularly relationships between young people and adults with a presence in relevant contexts, such as a school or sports club. These relationships flourish in wider contexts of safety – and could be undermined in contexts of harm. Indeed, as literature from the US and Europe indicated, when young people are in contexts that they experience as unsafe or controlling, this undermines their ability to form trusted relationships with professionals in those settings (Werkmeister Rozas et al, 2018; Aussems et al, 2020). Taken as a whole, therefore, a reflexive, rather than competitive, relationship can be seen between contextual and relational responses to EFRH.

Re-envisioning the social work role and definitions of vulnerability

In different ways, each of the five response characteristics presented in Chapters Three to Seven surfaces questions about whether more effective social care responses to EFRH can be achieved through the improvement of existing services, or whether a more fundamental rethinking of paradigms and systems is required. For example, would a better implementation of existing guidance and intervention models enable professionals to spend the time needed to build relationships with the young people they support, or is the only way to achieve this to disrupt the current status quo and redesign the system from scratch? For all five response characteristics, there are two system challenges that seem to prompt this question most – at least in a UK context.

The first of these is the extent to which conventional systems enable social workers to build relationships of trust and collaboration with young people, work effectively across agency boundaries, contribute to changing the contexts associated with EFRH, respond to the dynamics of EFRH and offer a youth-centred approach. Our review suggests that while improved implementation of existing policy, legislation and models is important, much of what is recommended in response to EFRH redefines how child and family social work in the UK has been framed or resourced. For example, recommendations for relational approaches (see Chapter Three) require system reforms that provide social work practitioners with reduced caseloads and more flexible timescales for intervention, and that position parents as partners in safeguarding (as opposed to being objects of concern). Similarly, the recommendation that social care responses address the contextual drivers of EFRH (see Chapter Five) requires systems that are designed to respond to groups and contexts directly, not just to individual young people and families – the way in which the system is largely configured currently.

A system redesign narrative is also evident in studies that recommend interagency responses to EFRH. Some of the UK literature highlights a changing interface between statutory agencies and the voluntary and community organisations that respond to EFRH. Up until 2015, voluntary sector organisations had been at the helm of responses to EFRH, as it was often not constituted as a safeguarding concern and did not meet the threshold for social work intervention. However, as the framing has shifted, questions are being asked about the remit of social care in EFRH. What should the role of a social worker in a statutory agency be with a young person at risk of harm beyond the home whose parents/carers are doing all they can to keep them safe? Moreover, if social workers in statutory agencies are now coordinating plans to support young people affected by EFRH, what is the remit of social workers in *voluntary* organisations? Furthermore, as calls are made for the police and wider criminal justice agencies to adopt a more welfare-based approach to adolescents in need of support, where does their contribution end and that of social care commence? Conversely, if social workers come to play a more central role in responding to crimes against young people, including exploitation, how does this remit differ from that played by criminal justice agencies? These questions reflect how the maturing and development of responses to EFRH are changing the ways in which systems and partnerships operate. The reconfiguration of the social work role in the UK that this entails goes far beyond incremental service improvement and implies policy and system transformation.

The second way in which this review indicates a need for system redesign is in respect of how services define those in need of support. As noted throughout this book – and detailed in Chapter Six – young people affected by EFRH may commit offences in the context of their own abuse or as a consequence of it. Some young people may be both victimised and victimising others at the same time. Yet, social care responses often operate on an assumed demarcation between victims and perpetrators, whether this results from statutory social work systems being built upon the idea that the state intervenes when children are let down or harmed by those responsible for their care, or whether it stems from voluntary organisations being framed as 'victim services' (Bruning and Doek, 2021).

There have been attempts to use legislative reform to create systems capable of holding victim–perpetrator overlaps, for example, in the UK and the US, which have redesignated 'child prostitution' (a form of crime committed by a young person) as CSE or domestic minor sex trafficking; here, changing the legislative basis has pushed services to consider young people's victimisation and vulnerability. However, this is not yet the case for young people who pose a risk of harm to others, rather than (or as well as) themselves – such as through involvement in drug trafficking or serious youth violence, which generally remain 'crimes'. Even countries like Scotland, which have more welfare-based youth justice systems, still struggle to build effective partnership responses to EFRH (Henderson et al, 2020). These dynamics of EFRH trouble the cultural, ethical and human elements of social care practice, and disrupt existing parameters of system configuration. Even with CSE, where there was less evidence from publications we reviewed that young people had been criminalised, victim-blaming narratives still emerged as a persistent challenge.

Across all five social care response characteristics, there appears to be an ongoing need for policy, service (re)design and practice to engage with complex, and somewhat contradictory, notions of adolescent 'vulnerability' to better accommodate these victim–perpetrator overlaps. Interagency working is often frustrated by the lack of shared definitions of who is in need of support, with disputes between the police and social care agencies being a particular point of contention. Contextual approaches to service design help professionals to situate young people's problematic behaviours within wider constraining conditions and respond accordingly. Youth-focused services also appear better able to accommodate the idea of 'imperfect' or 'agentic' victims: young people who are vulnerable and in need of support, while also acting and making decisions independently of adults. Revisiting the definition of 'vulnerability' seems central to supporting young people whose experiences of EFRH place them at the intersection of victim–perpetrator identities, particularly those who have aged out of the remit of child welfare services.

Mitigating the impact of structural drivers on social care responses

The review surfaced how the implementation of any of the five response characteristics can be undermined by structural drivers of harm. When austerity measures or other structural factors compromise the financial security of an organisation, the relationships (see Chapter Three) built through the practice interventions delivered by that organisation (and the intervention itself) are undermined. Interventions end prematurely, and in some cases, so does their impact. While many EFRH interventions engage with the contextual dynamics of such harm, they are negatively impacted by wider structural factors that are beyond their reach. Structural factors that are associated with EFRH (including poverty, employment and racism) and drive contextual factors (such as persistent neighbourhood violence and negative peer influences) compromise both organisational responses and practice interventions (see Chapter Five). Structural factors appear to drive specific dynamics of EFRH, particularly the creation of coercive and unsafe contexts in which young people have little access to protective and trusted services (see Chapter Six). Limited local support services emerge as a particular challenge for young people as they transition out of children's services; hence, there are calls for youth-centred responses capable of bridging the chasm between children's and adults' services for 18- to 25-year-olds (see Chapter Seven).

Far from being simply a target of intervention (see Chapter Five), structural drivers of EFRH need to be mitigated by social care systems themselves, lest they undermine the benefits of the five response characteristics presented in this book. Those who design, and deliver, social care systems need to consider whether their services (1) do enough to mitigate structural drivers of risk and (2) might exacerbate or create structural harm themselves. Commentators have cautioned against the unintended consequences of increasing the reach of statutory social care systems that monitor and scrutinise but offer little support to children and families (Featherstone et al, 2018). The oft-reported tensions in interagency working between social care and the police is a further example of this. Some social care responses that we reviewed challenged policing activity that criminalises, rather than supports, young people affected by EFRH, but in other studies, there was evidence that young people and/or families were sceptical of any real independence between law enforcement and social care agencies. If social care systems are experienced as punitive, disproportionally sanctioning or curtailing young people who are marginalised, then it will be very difficult (if not impossible) for those systems to successfully offer responses that are relational, contextual, youth centred or interagency, or that attend to the dynamics of EFRH.

The impact of structural factors on social care systems, and the potential for social care systems themselves to contribute to, or reinforce, those factors, takes us back to the question of whether (and to what extent) system redesign is required for responses to EFRH to be effective. To what extent does the culture of social care systems, and where they situate/ measure risk, harm and efficacy, require adaptation? Whether it is viewing young people affected by EFRH with reference to their experiences of poverty or inequality, or recognising that the harm young people cause others may be inextricably linked to their own victimisation, the existing cultures of social care responses in the UK and elsewhere appear to have their limits. Indeed, in many countries, issues such as child trafficking continue to be defined, and responded to, within criminal justice systems and are not always addressed as a separate child protection issue (Gregulska et al, 2020). Some of the successes of major system change, such as the reclassifying of child prostitution as CSE, may, in fact, be tied to a persisting individualised narrative of harm across a social care system still largely focused on responsibilising, treating and working with individual young people. Further-reaching reforms that draw in wider structural factors, be they legislative or practical, may require a cultural recalibration that social care systems are yet to achieve – even though individual practice interventions have sought to do so.

Figure 8.1: A framework for designing systems and improving responses to EFRH

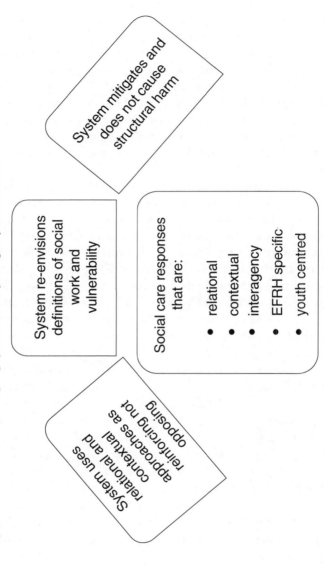

System mitigates and does not cause structural harm

System re-envisions definitions of social work and vulnerability

Social care responses that are:

- relational
- contextual
- interagency
- EFRH specific
- youth centred

System uses relational and contextual approaches as reinforcing not opposing

A framework for designing systems and improving responses to EFRH

The preceding chapters have detailed the five characteristics of promising or effective social care responses to EFRH that were identified through our review. In this chapter, we have presented three principles of social care systems that, we contend, are fundamental to the successful implementation of these characteristics: relational and contextual approaches should be recognised, and operationalised, as complementary rather than competing; some re-envisioning of how social work and vulnerability are defined will be required; and systems should seek to mitigate (rather than potentially contribute to) structural drivers of harm. Figure 8.1 illustrates the relationship between the five characteristics of social care responses and three principles of social care systems evidenced by our review as a framework for future system and service design.

This framework not only offers guidance for future system and service design, but also asks questions of existing systems and practices to assess the extent to which services in the UK, and in other international settings, align with the evidence base surfaced through this review (see Table 8.1). In the following, and closing, chapter, we signal some ways forward for applying this framework in the UK and beyond, noting where service and policy developments appear headed in the right direction and what may be outstanding.

Table 8.1: Questions to guide future system and service (re)design

	Response Characteristic 1 Relational	Response Characteristic 2 Contextual	Response Characteristic 3 Youth centred	Response Characteristic 4 Interagency	Response Characteristic 5 EFRH specific
System Principle 1 *View relational and contextual approaches as complementary*	Does the system provide contexts in which trusted relationships can be built and sustained?	Does the system establish/promote relationships with those who influence contexts associated with EFRH?	Does the system build safety in relationships and contexts that matter to young people?	Does the system feature relationships with individuals and organisations who can influence the nature of contexts where EFRH occurs?	Does the system build relationships around young people that encompass victim–perpetrator overlaps?
System Principle 2 *Re-envision how social work and vulnerability are defined*	Does the system create conditions for building trusting relationships between social workers and young people?	Does the system allow social workers to recognise and respond to vulnerable contexts and relationships, as well as individuals?	Does the system support collaborative practices between social workers and young people, enabling reconciliation between their agency, voice, rights, vulnerability and protection?	Are what constitutes vulnerability and the remit of professional roles agreed across the interagency system in ways that centre young people's welfare as paramount?	Does the system provide social work support to young people who pose, as well as face, risks, including beyond the age of 18?

	Response Characteristic 1 Relational	Response Characteristic 2 Contextual	Response Characteristic 3 Youth centred	Response Characteristic 4 Interagency	Response Characteristic 5 EFRH specific
System Principle 3 *Mitigate structural drivers of harm*	Does the system avoid short-term funding or intrusive data sharing that may compromise sustained relationships?	Does the system recognise and seek to address how such factors as poverty, racism and sexism intersect with, and inform, contextual dynamics of harm?	Does the system tailor approaches so as to meet the varying needs of young people by age, ethnicity, ability, sexuality and faith?	Does the system allow social care to challenge decisions that limit service provision for, and do not promote the welfare of, young people affected by EFRH?	Does the system allow social workers to challenge institutional drivers of EFRH, such as school exclusions and criminalisation?

NINE

New directions for the UK and beyond

Introduction

In this book, we have presented five characteristics associated with promising or effective responses to EFRH and the three principles of social care systems that are required for their successful operationalisation. However, to what extent are research and policy in the UK, and elsewhere, aligned with this evidence base? What further service improvement or system redesign is necessary to ensure young people experience social care responses that are reflective of the framework for designing systems and improving responses to EFRH presented in Chapter Eight?

In this final chapter, we identify directions of travel for research, policy and practice that will facilitate others in applying and advancing the work we have undertaken. In particular, we signal three broad challenges that require resolution: the nature of evidence; how adolescence is framed; and how services and sectors are organised around young people. The framework and associated questions for guiding future system and service design set out in Chapter Eight are nestled within these broader research, policy and service challenges, and their feasibility in practice will require their ongoing resolution. In considering these challenges, we close by noting that any progression of this work will likely require innovation and system transformation in respect of research, policy and service design, as well as incremental improvement within existing paradigms. We reflect on the need to achieve such transformation ethically, noting that system change is not in and of itself to the benefit of young people unless also grounded in principles of human rights, social justice and professional integrity (Hampson et al, 2021).

Looking back, moving forward

In Chapter One, we detailed the trajectory of research, policy and service responses to EFRH in the UK, and considered the alignment of such responses with other countries in the Global North. Reflecting on this trajectory, in light of the framework presented in Chapter Eight, we can see where research, policy or practice agendas currently reflect or enable the findings of our review, and where they warrant further attention. This applies to the nature of the evidence base available, broader narratives of adolescence and wider multi-sector systems in which responses to EFRH have been developed.

Evidence problems

From the outset, this review has been disruptive of existing paradigms and systems. It has engaged with a research evidence base that siloes forms of EFRH (CSE, criminal exploitation, radicalisation and so on) and, at an international level, lacks shared definitions for any individual form of EFRH, let alone an integrated category. Our review suggests that there is merit in both demarcation and integration, as well as in identifying points of intersection. We saw variance among commonalities, particularly in respect of responses to EFRH through exploitation or sexual abuse, as compared with EFRH associated with peers or criminality. These variances suggest caution around efforts to offer integrated accounts, but they also signal the potential pitfalls of not doing so, such as where approaches found beneficial for one type of EFRH are not considered for others. Why have relational and trauma-informed approaches to practice been evidenced as appropriate and helpful in situations of sexual exploitation but studied relatively little in peer abuse? And why have contextual interventions targeting peer and school norms been introduced, or recommended, in cases of peer abuse but underexplored in relation to sexual exploitation?

The review findings indicate that there is enough in common across social care responses to different forms of EFRH to warrant an integrated conceptualisation (see Chapter Two) and an associated service development framework (see Chapter Eight) – not only in the UK, where policy frameworks have been moving in this direction, but also in other international settings where systems struggle to engage with adolescence. However, at this stage, research and, to an extent, practice and policy remain siloed and do not offer the evidence base needed to build an international, integrated account of EFRH and associated social care responses. As such, the international transferability of some of the ideas presented in this book may be challenging. A first step would be for the questions set out in our framework to be sense-checked within other countries to determine the extent to which they are attuned to the policy and practice systems, and to any associated evidence base for social care responses to EFRH, that pertain within those countries. A second would involve raising the profile of EFRH within future international comparisons of child protection systems, so that the extent to which services targeting EFRH are included in the analysis is specified (or, if not, for services centred on adolescence to be at least demarcated). Without the introduction of a unified category in research, policy or practice, however, a unified response is less likely. The limitations of this study will also remain unaddressed, as persistent siloes will result in an evidence base too vast to manage by international review.

The adolescence 'problem'

Throughout this book, we have noted that challenges in responding to EFRH are themselves intertwined with wider system shortfalls in how adolescence has been conceptualised within research, policy and practice. The framework for future system and service design set out in Chapter Eight suggests that effective social care responses engage with the dynamics of adolescence on many fronts:

- They are youth centred, working with, rather than against, the dynamics of adolescent development, such as an increasing desire for autonomy (see Chapter Seven).
- They engage with contexts that increase in influence during adolescence compared to early childhood (such as public and peer settings) (see Chapter Five).
- They promote shared definitions of adolescent vulnerability across interagency partnerships (see Chapter Four).
- They have the agility to hold victim–perpetrator overlaps for young people who do not fit stereotyped presentations of victimhood (see Chapter Six).
- They provide young people with relationships built on trust that they can opt into when the time is right (see Chapter Three).

In short, effective responses to EFRH are impossible without due consideration to how systems engage with the dynamics of adolescence. Yet, throughout this book, we have noted how systems in the UK, and in various other international settings, seem to continually struggle with this period of human development. The use of out-of-home care and the rate at which young people go missing from such placements (see Chapters One, Six and Seven), or the restrictions placed on young people's liberty as a means of creating a physical distance between them and the contexts/relationships in which they come to harm (see Chapter Three), all signal *control* used as a means of care. At the other end of the spectrum, we see young people held responsible for the harm they experience and social care responses and legislative frameworks being mobilised to push against victim-blaming narratives (see Chapters One, Seven and Eight) – narratives that are themselves used differentially against young people who are racialised, impoverished or discriminated against in other ways.

Efforts to control or blame young people for what they are experiencing are all symptomatic of a poor fit between the nature of adolescence and protective systems. Research has not always aided developments either. Much literature on international child protection systems, including those that are comparative, fail to differentiate how those systems respond to adolescents compared with younger children, clouding opportunities to identify points of similarity and difference in how effective services are designed.

In Chapter Eight, we noted that our framework for designing systems and improving responses to EFRH could only be implemented successfully within a wider system that has re-envisioned what 'vulnerability' means so that young people do not lose rights to autonomy, voice or protection. The feasibility of our framework is itself tied to the ability of social care systems to engage with the dynamics of adolescence.

System and service problems

Finally, while our review was focused on social care responses, approaches seeking to address EFRH can be found within a range of other sectors, including health, youth justice and youth work. Forms of EFRH, and the practice and system responses to them, are not only studied across disparate disciplines, including criminology, sociology, psychology, social work, social geography, youth studies and so on, but also cut across variable (and sometimes incompatible) legislative frameworks and associated professional systems. Our framework for designing systems and improving responses is built on the premise that EFRH presents a risk of significant harm to young people and, as such, requires professional responses led by social care. Yet, social care leadership in the field of EFRH, particularly in statutory social work settings, is relatively young in the UK and largely underdeveloped elsewhere. As was illustrated in Chapter One, despite certain policy changes, much of the UK's response to EFRH remains within a criminal justice and community safety framework (though this is much less the case for EFRH involving sexual harm, particularly CSE). Internationally, many of the issues discussed in this book are viewed principally through the lens of youth justice and, to varying degrees, youth work. The framework produced by this review invites us to rethink the relationship between social care and public protection, youth justice, and community safety, asking not only which one would be best positioned to lead responses to EFRH, but also how systems may balance the competing demands of those policy and practice frameworks.

Applying principles of ethical innovation to improving and transforming responses

The efficacy of the framework we have presented to guide the improvement or (re)design of systems and service responses to EFRH, and to shape the study of those systems, is somewhat dependent upon finding resolutions to the three challenges outlined in the preceding section. In this sense, the operationalisation of our framework is likely to require an unsettling of existing paradigms and transformative change (innovation) in system design and practice approaches, rather than more incremental forms of service improvement. The level of change required, and how disruptive this needs to be, depends on the specific contexts of protection systems and practices, and their underlying values, shaped as they are by policy and legislative frameworks that differ across countries and political systems, as well as by local factors and contexts, including organisational cultures and relationships, and the level and quality of interagency working.

Such disruptive and transformative change has already started to occur in the UK, where the shifts towards a more integrated conceptualisation of EFRH, and the identification of these risks and harms during adolescence as a safeguarding issue that should be addressed, first and foremost, through child protection and social welfare legislation, deserve recognition. Moreover, there has been investment in the UK by central government, research councils and charities in the piloting and scale-up of new interventions and practice systems to address EFRH, such approaches include complex safeguarding (Firmin et al, 2019), those developed by this book's first author, that is, contextual safeguarding (Firmin et al, 2016), as well as trauma-informed practice (Hickle, 2020) and transitional safeguarding (Holmes and Smale, 2018), all of which are attuned to key elements of our framework outlined in Chapter Eight. *Innovation* rather than improvement has been the key policy and conceptual frame underpinning many of these new approaches and concepts. A paper co-written by this book's second author analyses the specific conditions affecting innovation endeavours in children's social care in the UK over the past decade or so; in this, the authors identify shifts and disruptions at the level of power and relationships, and in respect of how risks are framed, understood and worked with, as crucial domains for the processes of undoing and redoing that characterise innovation:

> Collaborative and participative relationships help to disrupt existing dynamics of power, agency and status and allow a trusting foundation from which to explore uncertainty. ... Disciplined approaches to experimentation that allow managed risk-taking can create the space for different kinds of relationships to emerge and question the distribution of power and role of social justice within the system ... shifting power closer to young people and families allows them to exercise their rights, to take

control of the relationships that are central to their lives, and to explore possibilities for change within them. (Hampson et al, 2021: 203)

The three key principles that Hampson et al (2021) outline as fundamental to ethical innovation in social care – human rights, social justice and professional integrity – are also central to any processes that work towards creating more effective responses for addressing EFRH. These principles draw on the ethics and value statements of the International Federation of Social Workers (IFSW, 2018) and professional associations in different countries (for the UK, see BASW, 2014), and therefore provide a guiding framework for initiating, implementing and evaluating change across contexts.

Incorporating human rights principles into service responses

Social work's commitment to human rights principles and related values involves upholding every person's dignity and well-being, respecting their right to self-determination, promoting their participation rights, and working holistically with people and their social systems and contexts, while also focusing on their capacity and strengths (BASW, 2014). Conceptualising EFRH as breaches of young people's human rights involves viewing these rights holistically, that is, as duties enshrined in international law (and implemented into national legal and policy contexts). These duties involve protecting, fulfilling and realising human rights proactively, rather than simply avoiding or sanctioning breaches of rights – an understanding that is highly compatible with the five characteristics and three overarching principles set out in Chapter Eight. It is clear that the criminalisation of young people in the context of EFRH would be incompatible with such an understanding of human rights duties. However, in practice (as noted in Chapter One), diverging legal definitions of child abuse and exploitation, shifting thresholds for service provision, and ambivalence about which agencies should take a lead in safeguarding adolescents impacted by CSE or trafficking may result in many young people (particularly over the age of 18) falling through child protection nets and/or being criminalised – as they are in the US and several countries across Europe (Degani et al, 2015; Pullmann et al, 2020).

Transforming systems and practices in line with social justice concerns

To be consonant with the statements of ethical principles for social work at the UK and international levels (BASW, 2014; IFSW, 2018), system and service improvements and innovation need to align with social justice concerns (Hampson et al, 2021). As discussed in Chapter One, services for young people in the UK have been disproportionately affected by cuts as part of austerity policies over the past decade, and this continues to affect endeavours to innovate and transform responses to EFRH, along with the increased exposure of existing inequalities through the COVID-19 pandemic. Such tensions and system pressures are faced by the social work profession internationally (Lorenz, 2017; Ornellas et al, 2019). In these contexts, a shift towards rationalised targeted interventions, the intersection of social care responses with those from other sectors (such as housing, mental health or criminal justice), the inherent short-termism of policy and practice initiatives, and the slow or sometimes even retrograde progress in understanding the nature of EFRH during adolescence – which we have detailed across this book – all provide barriers to the transformative innovation needed to achieve more effective responses. At the same time, they also point us to key areas where such change is most needed.

Prioritising young people's voices

Finally, despite the increased recognition internationally of the need to ensure meaningful participation of young people and families, their voices are still not adequately heard in informing responses to EFRH. We still know relatively little about young people's perceptions and experiences, not only of risk and harm beyond the home, but also of what counts as safety in the various contexts and relationships in their lives. International comparative research in social work tends to focus on vulnerable young people at a macro-level of analysis but often fails to look at the multiple facets of young people's lives and how these might shape vulnerabilities or build protective factors (Healy et al, 2011). This is in spite of the small body of literature concerned with participatory research and practice with young people who have experienced EFRH which suggests that young people are both willing and capable of informing responses (see Cody, 2017; Bovarnick et al, 2018).

In ending this book, we return to Child Q and other young people like her who have clearly articulated their rights to be, and feel, safe in contexts beyond their homes. The risks some young people may be exposed to, and the harms this may cause, often require more in response than existing systems have been designed to offer. We have drawn together a disparate evidence base to understand what an enhanced social care offer needs to entail and developed a framework to guide future system improvement and transformation. This framework, and the associated critical questions, will likely require adaptation as learning in this field develops and as young people are engaged in the testing and evaluation of new or enhanced services. For now, it offers a place to anchor efforts to build integrated, ethical and effective social care responses to EFRH.

Glossary

Child criminal exploitation In the UK, this is defined as where a child or young person under the age of 18 (or a vulnerable adult) is coerced, manipulated or deceived into criminal activity (1) in exchange for something the victim needs or wants and/or (2) for the financial advantage or increased status of the perpetrator or facilitator. It can occur either through physical contact or the use of technology.

Child protection This refers to a legal set of duties carried out by systems and practitioners to protect individual children identified as suffering or likely to suffer significant (serious) harm. It is part of the wider safeguarding role.

Child sexual exploitation (CSE) In the UK, this is defined as where a child or young person under the age of 18 (or a vulnerable adult) is coerced, manipulated or deceived into sexual activity (1) in exchange for something the victim needs or wants and/or (2) for the financial advantage or increased status of the perpetrator or facilitator. It can occur either through physical contact or the use of technology.

County Lines A form of criminal exploitation where gangs and organised criminal networks draw on children, young people and vulnerable adults to move illegal drugs around different counties of the UK, using dedicated mobile phone lines. Coercion, intimidation and actual or threatened physical and sexual violence commonly feature to secure young people's compliance.

Domestic Minor Sex Trafficking In US law, this covers the recruitment, harbouring, transportation or provision of children for sexual activity when this occurs within the borders of a country.

Extra-familial risks and harms (EFRH) This refers to dangerous or harmful contexts and situations involving peers and adults unconnected to young people's families or homes, which may be associated with exploitation, abuse or criminality, and that raise safeguarding concerns. Examples include: sexual and criminal exploitation and trafficking; peer-to-peer sexual and relational abuse; serious physical violence between young people, including weapon-enabled violence; and radicalisation.

Harmful sexual behaviours Inappropriate or abusive behaviour of a sexual nature displayed by children and young people, either to peers, younger children or adults.

Interagency/multi-agency The terms 'multi-agency', 'interagency' and 'interdisciplinary' are used interchangeably to refer to any collaboration between agencies or between professionals from different agencies.

Local safeguarding children boards These were the key statutory mechanism in England for agreeing and coordinating how the relevant organisations in each local area should cooperate to safeguard and promote the welfare of children. They were replaced in 2019 with new local safeguarding arrangements, as set out in the Children and Social Work Act 2017.

Modern slavery/trafficking The serious and illegal exploitation of other people for personal or commercial gain.

It includes sexual and criminal exploitation, human trafficking, and domestic servitude and forced labour.

Peer-to-peer abuse Includes physical and sexual abuse, harassment and violence, as well as bullying, emotional harm and teenage relationship abuse. It may take place online and offline, and may extend to involvement in grooming other children for exploitation.

Radicalisation The process by which a person comes to support extremist ideologies (generally political or religious in nature) and becomes associated with terrorist groups or activities. The risk of physical or emotional harm that might result for those subject to radicalisation, as well as the risk posed to others, is a safeguarding consideration.

Safeguarding This is defined broadly in the UK as a collective responsibility to protect people's health, well-being and human rights, and enabling them to live free from harm, abuse and neglect. Within the Children Act 1989 (in England and Wales) and subsequent statutory guidance, safeguarding encompasses actions taken to promote the welfare of children and protect them from harm. 'Child protection' is a subset of safeguarding, referring to systems and roles dedicated to assessing and addressing risks and harms for young people under the age of 18, largely through interventions focused on parenting. For adults, statutory guidance under the Care Act 2014 describes safeguarding as protecting an adult's right to live in safety, free from abuse and neglect, including risk prevention.

Serious case reviews These were the statutory mechanism by which local multi-agency safeguarding networks in England considered points of learning arising from instances of child abuse or neglect that have led to death or serious harm. These have been superseded by child safeguarding practice reviews. The term 'serious case reviews' is used in Scotland, 'child practice reviews' in Wales and 'case management reviews' in Northern Ireland. Where there have been failures to protect a young person over 18 from harm and abuse, a safeguarding adults review provides a similar mechanism.

Serious youth violence In the UK, this refers to serious violence and assault, potentially with a weapon, such as a knife, and where a young person under the age of 20 is injured. It could include murder, manslaughter, rape, wounding with intent and causing grievous bodily harm.

Social care This is an umbrella term used within the UK to encompass the provision or brokering of services related to the care, protection or social or emotional support of children or adults defined (within primary legislation) as being in need of those services and/or at risk of harm without them (SCIE, 2012). We have used this broad definition to cover services and interventions delivered by organisations and practitioners within statutory, voluntary (non-profit) and community sectors to respond to EFRH.

Young people These are individuals who are subject to, or involved with, the services for EFRH that are discussed in this book. Our broad definition of adolescence means that this includes children and young adults from the ages of 12 to 25. Although in UK legislation, the term 'child' encompasses young people up to the age of 18, we reserve the use of child in this book to refer to those below the age of 12.

References

Alexander, T.M. and Enns, J.T. (1988) 'Age changes in the boundaries of fuzzy categories', *Child Development*, 599(5): 1372–86.

All-Party Parliamentary Group for Runaway and Missing Children and Adults (2017) *Briefing Report on the Roundtable on Children Who Go Missing and Are Criminally Exploited by Gangs*. London: Missing People.

Anderson, M. and Parkinson, K. (2018) 'Balancing justice and welfare needs in family group conferences for children with harmful sexual behavior: the HSB-FGC framework', *Journal of Child Sexual Abuse*, 27(5): 490–509.

Annie E. Casey Foundation (2022) 'What are status offenses and why do they matter?', 6 April. Available at: www.aecf.org/blog/what-are-status-offenses-and-why-do-they-matter (accessed 11 May 2022).

Association of Directors of Children's Services (2019) *Serious Youth Violence and Knife Crime: ADCS Discussion Paper*. Manchester: Association of Directors of Children's Services.

Astrup, J. (2019) 'Knife crime: where's the public health approach?', *Community Practitioner*, 92(6): 14–17.

Aussems, K., Muntinga, M., Addink, A., and Dedding, C. (2020) ' "Call us by our name": quality of care and wellbeing from the perspective of girls in residential care facilities who are commercially and sexually exploited by "loverboys"', *Children and Youth Services Review*, 116: 105213.

Barker, B., Kerr, T., Nguyen, P., Wood, E. and DeBeck, K. (2015) 'Barriers to health and social services for street-involved youth in a Canadian setting', *Journal of Public Health Policy*, 36(3): 350–63.

BASW (British Association of Social Workers) (2014) *The BASW Code of Ethics for Social Work*. Birmingham: British Association of Social Workers.

Beatriz, E., Lincoln, A., Alder, J., Daley, N., Simmons, F., Ibeh, K., Figueroa, C. and Molnar, B. (2018) 'Evaluation of a teen dating violence prevention intervention among urban middle-school youth using youth participatory action research: lessons learned from Start Strong Boston', *Journal of Family Violence*, 33(8): 563–78.

Bedford, A. (2015) *Serious Case Review into Child Sexual Exploitation in Oxfordshire: From the Experiences of Children A, B, C, D, E, and F*. Oxford: Oxfordshire Safeguarding Children Board.

Benavente, B., Díaz-Faes, D.A., Ballester, L. and Pereda, N. (2021) 'Commercial sexual exploitation of children and adolescents in Europe: a systematic review', *Trauma, Violence, & Abuse*: 1–20.

Berelowitz, S., Firmin, C., Edwards, G. and Gulyurtlu, S. (2012) *'I Thought I Was the Only One. The Only One in the World': The Office of the Children's Commissioner's Inquiry into Child Sexual Exploitation in Gangs and Groups Interim Report*. London: Office of the Children's Commissioner.

Berelowitz, S., Ritchie, D.G. and Edwards, G. (2015) *'if It's Not Better, It's Not the End': Inquiry into Child Sexual Exploitation in Gangs and Groups: One Year on*. London: Office of the Children's Commissioner.

Berry, L.J., Tully, R.J. and Egan, V. (2017) 'A case study approach to reducing the risks of child sexual exploitation (CSE)', *Journal of Child Sexual Abuse*, 26(7): 769–84.

Big Lottery Fund (2018) *Preventing Serious Youth Violence: What Works? Insights and Examples from the Community and Voluntary Sector*. London: Big Lottery Fund.

Black, B., Weisz, A.N. and Jayasundara, D.S. (2012) 'Dating violence and sexual assault prevention with African American middle schoolers: does group gender composition impact dating violence attitudes?', *Child & Youth Services*, 33(2): 158–73.

Boddy, J., Statham, J., McQuail, S., Petrie, P. and Owen, C. (2009) *Working at the 'Edges' of Care? European Models of Support for Young People and Families*. London: Thomas Coram Research Unit, Institute of Education.

Boulton, L.J., Phythian, R. and Kirby, S. (2019) 'Diverting young men from gangs: a qualitative evaluation', *Policing*, 42(5): 887–900.

Bounds, D., Otwell, C., Melendez, A., Karnik, N. and Julion, W. (2020) 'Adapting a family intervention to reduce risk factors for sexual exploitation', *Child and Adolescent Psychiatry and Mental Health*, 14(1).

Bovarnick, S., Peace, D., Warrington, C. and Pearce, J.J. (2018) *Being Heard: Promoting Children and Young People's Involvement in Participatory Research on Sexual Violence: Findings from an International Scoping Review*. Luton: University of Bedfordshire.

Brandon, M., Sidebotham, P., Belderson, P., Cleaver, H., Dickens, J., Garstang, J., Harris, J., Sorensen, P. and Wate, R. (2020) *Complexity and Challenge: A Triennial Analysis of SCRs 2014–2017*. London: Department for Education.

Brown, K. (2019) 'Vulnerability and child sexual exploitation: towards an approach grounded in life experiences', *Critical Social Policy*, 39(4): 622–42.

Bruning, M.R. and Doek, J. (2021) 'Characteristics of an effective child protection system in the European and international contexts', *International Journal on Child Maltreatment: Research, Policy and Practice*, 4(3): 231–56.

Bulanda, J.J. and McCrea, K.T. (2013) 'The promise of an accumulation of care: disadvantaged African-American youths' perspectives about what makes an after school program meaningful', *Child & Adolescent Social Work Journal*, 30(2): 95–118.

Child Safeguarding Practice Review Panel (2020) *It Was Hard to Escape: Safeguarding Children at Risk from Criminal Exploitation*. London: Department for Education.

Children and Young People's Centre for Justice (2021) *A Guide to Youth Justice in Scotland: Policy, Practice and Legislation.* Glasgow: CYCJ.

Chisholm, T. and Coulter, A. (2017) *Safeguarding and Radicalisation: Research Report.* London: Department for Education.

Christie, C. (2018) *A Trauma-Informed Health and Care Approach for Responding to Child Sexual Abuse and Exploitation: Current Knowledge Report.* London: Chanon Consulting.

Clements, K., Holmes, D., Ryder, R. and Mortimer, E. (2017) *Workforce Perspectives on Harmful Sexual Behaviour: Findings from the Local Authorities Research Consortium 7.* London: National Children's Bureau.

Cockbain, E. and Brayley, H. (2012) 'Child sexual exploitation and youth offending: a research note', *European Journal of Criminology,* 9(6): 689–700.

Cody, C. (2017) '"We have personal experience to share, it makes it real": young people's views on their role in sexual violence prevention effort', *Children and Youth Services Review,* 79: 221–7.

Coffey, A. (2014) *Real Voices: Child Sexual Exploitation in Greater Manchester. An Independent Report by Ann Coffey, MP.* Manchester: It's Not Okay.

Coker, A.L. Bush, H.M., Cook-Craig, P.G., DeGue, S.A., Clear, E.R., Brancato, C.J., Fisher, B.S. and Recktenwald, E.A. (2017) 'RCT testing bystander effectiveness to reduce violence', *American Journal of Preventive Medicine,* 52(5): 566–78.

Coomer, R. and Moyle, L. (2017) 'The changing shape of street-level heroin and crack supply in England: commuting, holidaying and cuckooing drug dealers across "County Lines"', *British Journal of Criminology,* 58: 1323–42.

Cordis Bright (2019) *Evaluation of the Disrupting Exploitation Programme – Year 1 Report: Executive Summary.* London: Cordis Bright.

Countryman-Roswurm, K. and Bolin, B.L. (2014) 'Domestic minor sex trafficking: assessing and reducing risk', *Child & Adolescent Social Work Journal,* 31(6): 521–38.

Coy, M. (2017) 'All Fired Up Now': The Safe Choices Leaving Care and Custody Project Programme on Sexual Exploitation: Final Evaluation Report. London: London Metropolitan University.

Crawford, C., Boyd, C., Jain, S., Khorsah, R. and Jonas, W. (2015) 'Rapid evidence assessment of the literature (REAL©): streamlining the systematic review process and creating utility for evidence-based health care', BMC Research Notes, 8(631), DOI: 10.1186/s13104-015-1604-z.

D'Arcy, K. and Thomas, R. (2016) Nightwatch: CSE in Plain Sight. Final Evaluation Report. Luton: University of Bedfordshire.

Davis, J. (2019) Safeguarding Black Girls from Child Sexual Abuse: Messages from Research. London: Community Care Inform.

Davis, J. and Marsh, N. (2020) 'Boys to men: the cost of "adultification" in safeguarding responses to Black boys', Critical and Radical Social Work, 8(2): 255–9.

De Pedro, K.T., Lynch, R.J. and Esqueda, M.C. (2018) 'Understanding safety, victimization and school climate among rural lesbian, gay, bisexual, transgender, and questioning (LGBTQ) youth', Journal of LGBT Youth, 15(4): 265–79.

Degani, P., Pividori, C. and Bufo, M. (eds) (2015) Trafficked and Exploited Minors between Vulnerability and Illegality. Osservatorio Interventi Tratta.

Department for Children, Schools and Families (2009) Safeguarding Children and Young People from Sexual Exploitation. London: HMSO.

Department for Education (2021) 'Children's social care innovation programme: insights and evaluation'. Available at: www.gov.uk/guidance/childrens-social-care-innovation-programme-insights-and-evaluation#history (accessed 11 May 2022).

Department for Education and Skills (2007) Targeted Youth Support: A Guide. London: DfES.

Department of Health (2017) 'Co-operating to safeguard children and young people in Northern Ireland'. Available at: www.health-ni.gov.uk/publications/co-operating-safeguard-children-and-young-people-northern-ireland (accessed 11 May 2022).

Eaton, J. and Holmes, D. (2017) *Working Effectively to Address Child Sexual Exploitation: Evidence Scope*. Dartington: Research in Practice.

Estyn (2021) *'We Don't Tell Our Teachers.' Experiences of Peer-on-Peer Sexual Harassment among Secondary School Pupils in Wales*. Cardiff: Estyn.

Fagan, A.A. and Catalano, R.F. (2013) 'What works in youth violence prevention', *Research on Social Work Practice*, 23(2): 141–56.

Farrell, A., Lockwood, S., Goggin, K. and Hogan, S. (2019) *Specialized Residential Placements for Child Trafficking Victims*. Boston: Northeastern University

Featherstone, B., Gupta, A., Morris, K. and White, S. (2018) *Protecting Children: A Social Model*. Bristol: Policy Press.

Firmin, C. (2020) *Contextual Safeguarding and Child Protection: Rewriting the Rules*. Oxford: Routledge.

Firmin, C. and Rayment-McHugh, S. (2020) 'Two roads, one destination: Community and organizational mechanisms for contextualizing child abuse prevention in Australia and the UK', *International Journal on Child Maltreatment: Research, Policy and Practice*, 3(2): 229.

Firmin, C., Warrington, C. and Pearce, J. (2016) 'Sexual exploitation and its impact on developing sexualities and sexual relationships: the need for contextual social work interventions', *British Journal of Social Work*, 46(8): 2318–37.

Firmin, C., Horan, J., Holmes, D. and Hopper, G. (2019) *Safeguarding during Adolescence: The Relationship between Contextual Safeguarding, Complex Safeguarding and Transitional Safeguarding*. Devon: Research in Practice.

FitzSimons, A. and McCracken, K. (2020) *Children's Social Care Innovation Programme: Round 2 Final Report*. London: Department for Education.

Fong, R. and Cardoso, J.B. (2010) 'Child human trafficking victims: challenges for the child welfare system', *Evaluation and Program Planning*, 33(3): 311–16.

Foshee, V.A., McNaughton Reyes, L., Agnew-Brune, C.B., Simon, T.R., Vaji, K.V., Lee, R.D. and Suchindran, C. (2014) 'The effects of the evidence-based Safe Dates dating abuse prevention program on other youth violence outcomes', *Prevention Science*, 15(6): 907–16.

Foster, R. (2013) *Knife Crime Interventions: 'What Works?'*. Glasgow: The Scottish Centre for Crime and Justice Research.

Franklin, A. and Smeaton, E. (2017) 'Recognising and responding to young people with learning disabilities who experience, or are at risk of, child sexual exploitation in the UK', *Children and Youth Services Review*, 73: 474–81.

Frost, N. (2017) 'From "silo" to "network" profession – a multi-professional future for social work', *Journal of Children's Services*, 12(2–3): 174–83.

Gamble, J. and McCallum, R. (2022) 'Local child safeguarding practice review: Child Q', City & Hackney Safeguarding Children Partnership. Available at: https://chscp.org.uk/wp-content/uplo ads/2022/03/Child-Q-PUBLISHED-14-March-22.pdf (accessed 30 May 2022).

Gibbs, A., Jewkes, R., Sikweyiya, Y. and Willan, S. (2015) 'Reconstructing masculinity? A qualitative evaluation of the Stepping Stones and Creating Futures interventions in urban informal settlements in South Africa', *Culture, Health & Sexuality*, 17(2): 208–22.

Gibbs, D.A., Hardison Walters, J.L., Lutnick, A., Miller, S. and Kluckman, M. (2015) 'Services to domestic minor victims of sex trafficking: opportunities for engagement and support', *Children and Youth Services Review*, 54: 1–7.

Gilbert, N., Parton, N. and Skivenes, M. (eds) (2011) *Child Protection Systems: International Trends and Orientations*. Oxford: Oxford University Press.

Goldenberg, S., Engstrom, D., Rolon, M.L., Silverman, J. and Strathdee, S. (2013) 'Sex workers' perspectives on strategies to reduce sexual exploitation and HIV risk: a qualitative study in Tijuana, Mexico', *PloS One*, 8(8): e72982.

Greenhalgh, T. and Peacock, R. (2005) 'Effectiveness and efficiency of search methods in systematic reviews of complex evidence: audit of primary sources', *BMJ*, 331: 1064.

Gregulska, J.H., Healy, C., Makulec, A., Petreska, E., Safin, D. and Smetek, J. (2020) *Study on Reviewing the Functioning of Member States' National and Transnational Referral Mechanisms.* Luxembourg: European Commission Publications Office.

Grunwald, K. and Thiersch, H. (2009) 'The concept of the "lifeworld orientation" for social work and social care', *Journal of Social Work Practice*, 23(2): 131–46.

Gutierrez, C.O. and Chawla, S. (2017) *The Child Sexual Exploitation of Young South Asian Women in Birmingham and Coventry.* London: The Children's Society.

Hallett, S. (2015) '"An uncomfortable comfortableness": "care", child protection and child sexual exploitation', *British Journal of Social Work*, 46(7): 2137–52.

Hämäläinen, J. (2015) 'Defining social pedagogy: historical, theoretical and practical considerations', *The British Journal of Social Work*, 45(3): 1022–38.

Hampson, M., Goldsmith, C. and Lefevre, M. (2021) 'Towards a framework for ethical innovation in children's social care', *Journal of Children's Services*, 16(3): 198–213.

Hanson, E. and Holmes, D. (2014) *That Difficult Age: Developing a More Effective Response to Risks in Adolescence: Evidence Scope.* Totness: Research in Practice.

Hardy, V.L., Compton, K.D. and McPhatter, V.S. (2013) 'Domestic minor sex trafficking: practice implications for mental health professionals', *Affilia: Journal of Women & Social Work*, 28(1): 8–18.

Healy, K., Lundström, T. and Sallnäs, M. (2011) 'A comparison of out-of-home care for children and young people in Australia and Sweden: worlds apart?', *Australian Social Work*, 64(4), 416–31.

Henderson, G., Kurlus, I. and Parry, R. (2020) *Sexual Exploitation of Children Involved in the Children's Hearings System*, Glasgow: Barnardo's and the Children's Reporter.

Hickle, K. (2020) 'Introducing a trauma-informed capability approach in youth services', *Children & Society*, 34(6): 537–51.

Hickle, K. and Lefevre, M. (2022) 'Learning to love and trust again: a relational approach to developmental trauma', in D. Holmes (ed) *Safeguarding Young People: Risk, Rights, Relationships and Resilience.* London: Jessica Kingsley, pp 159–76.

Her Majesty's Government (2005) *Youth Matters.* London: Her Majesty's Stationery Office.

Her Majesty's Government (2018) *Working Together to Safeguard Children: A Guide to Inter-Agency Working to Safeguard and Promote the Welfare of Children.* London: Stationary Office.

Holmes, D. (2022) 'Transitional safeguarding: the case for change', *Practice,* 34(1): 7–23.

Holmes, D. and Smale, E. (2018) *Transitional Safeguarding – Adolescence to Adulthood.* Devon: Research in Practice and Research in Practice for Adults.

Home Affairs Select Committee (2019) *Serious Youth Violence: Sixteenth Report of Session 2017–19.* London: House of Commons.

Hudek, J. (2018a) *County Lines: Scoping Report.* London: St Giles Trust.

Hudek, J. (2018b) *Evaluation of County Lines Pilot Project.* London: St Giles Trust.

Hughes, K., Hardcastle, K. and Perkins C. (2015) *A Review of Interventions to Improve Mental Health and Wellbeing of Gang-Affiliated Young People: A Rapid Evidence Synthesis.* London: Public Health England.

IFSW (International Federation of Social Workers) (2018) 'Global social work statement of ethical principles'. Available at: www.ifsw.org/global-social-work-statement-of-ethical-principles/ (accessed 28 May 2022).

Independent Anti-Slavery Commissioner (2022) *Annual Report 2021–2022.* London: Her Majesty's Stationery Office.

Institute of Public Care (2015) 'Hampshire County Council, supporting children and young people at risk of sexual exploitation: rapid research review'. Available at: www.education.ox.ac.uk/wp-content/uploads/2019/06/Young-People-at-Risk-of-Sexual-Exploitation-Hampshire.pdf (accessed 28 May 2022).

Jago, S., Arocha, L., Brodie, I., Melrose, M., Pearce, J.J. and Warrington, C. (2011) *What's Going on to Safeguard Children and Young People from Sexual Exploitation? How Local Partnerships Respond to Child Sexual Exploitation.* Luton: University of Bedfordshire.

Jay, A (2014) *Independent Inquiry into Child Sexual Exploitation in Rotherham.* Rotherham: Rotherham Metropolitan Borough Council.

Josenhans, V., Kavenagh, M., Smith, S. and Wekerle, C. (2020) 'Gender, rights and responsibilities: the need for a global analysis of the sexual exploitation of boys', *Child Abuse & Neglect*, 110: 104291.

Kernsmith, P.D. and Hernandez-Jozefowicz, D.M. (2011) 'A gender-sensitive peer education program for sexual assault prevention in the schools', *Children and Schools*, 33(3): 146–57.

Kirkman, M. (2020) *Policy Report: Sexual Exploitation of Children Involved in the Children's Hearings System.* Glasgow: Barnardo's.

Kohli, R.K.S., Hynes, P., Connolly, H., Thurnham, A., Westlake, D. and D'Arcy, K. (2015) *Evaluation of Independent Child Trafficking Advocates Trial: Final Report.* London: Home Office.

Lady Hale (2019) '30 years of the Children Act 1989 – Scarman Lecture 2019', Law Commission, 13 November. Available at: www.supremecourt.uk/docs/speech-191113.pdf (accessed 27 May 2022).

Langhinrichsen-Rohling, J. and Turner, L.A. (2012) 'The efficacy of an intimate partner violence prevention program with high-risk adolescent girls: a preliminary test', *Prevention Science*, 13(4): 384–94.

Latzman, N.E., Gibbs, D.A., Feinberg, R., Kluckman, M.N. and Aboul-Hosn, S. (2019) 'Human trafficking victimization among youth who run away from foster care', *Children and Youth Services Review*, 98: 113–24.

Lefevre, M., Hickle, K., Luckock, B. and Ruch, G. (2017) 'Building trust with children and young people at risk of child sexual exploitation: the professional challenge', *British Journal of Social Work*, 47(8): 2456–73.

Lefevre, M., Hickle, K. and Luckock, B. (2019) '"Both/and" not "either/or": reconciling rights to protection and participation in working with child sexual exploitation', *British Journal of Social Work*, 49(7): 1837–55.

Lefevre, M., Preston, O., Hickle, K., Horan, R., Drew, H., Banerjee, R., Cane, T., Barrow, M. and Bowyer, S. (2020) *Evaluation of the Implementation of a Contextual Safeguarding System in the London Borough of Hackney*. London: Department for Education.

Leon, L. and Raws, P. (2016) *Boys Don't Cry: Improving Identification and Disclosure of Sexual Exploitation among Boys and Young Men Trafficked to the UK*. London: The Children's Society.

Letourneau, E.J., Schaeffer, C.M., Bradshaw, C.P. and Feder, K.A. (2017) 'Preventing the onset of child sexual abuse by targeting young adolescents with universal prevention programming', *Child Maltreatment*, 22(2): 100–11.

Liles, B.D., Blacker, D.M., Landini, J.L. and Urquiza, A.J. (2016) 'A California multidisciplinary juvenile court: serving sexually exploited and at-risk youth', *Behavioral Sciences & the Law*, 34(1): 234–45.

Lloyd, J. (2018) 'Abuse through sexual image sharing in schools: response and responsibility', *Gender and Education*, 32(6): 784–802.

Lloyd, J. (2019) 'Response and interventions into harmful sexual behaviour in schools', *Child Abuse & Neglect*, 94: 104037.

Lloyd, J. and Firmin, C. (2020) 'No further action: contextualising social care decisions for children victimised in extra-familial settings', *Youth Justice*, 20(1–2): 79–92.

Lloyd, J., Walker, J. and Firmin, C. (2020) 'Keeping children safe? Advancing social care assessments to address harmful sexual behaviour in schools', *Child and Family Social Work*, 25(4): 751–60.

Lorenz, W. (2017) 'European policy developments and their impact on social work', *European Journal of Social Work*, 20(1): 17–28.

Luke, N. (2017) *Child Sexual Exploitation and Mental Health: Children's Social Care Innovation Programme, Thematic Report 3*. London: Department for Education.

REFERENCES

Lumos (2020) *Crack in the System: Child Trafficking in the Context of Institutional Care in Europe*. London: Lumos Foundation.

Lushey, C., Hyde-Dryden, G., Holmes, L. and Blackmore, J. (2017) *Evaluation of the No Wrong Door Innovation Programme (Research Report 51)*. London: Department for Education.

MacAlister, J. (2021) 'The case for change: the Independent Review of Children's Social Care'. Available at: https://childrenssocialcare. independent-review.uk/case-for-change/ (accessed 29 May 2022).

MacAlister, J. (2022) 'The Independent Review of Children's Social Care: final report'. Available at: https://childrenssocialcare.inde pendent-review.uk/ (accessed 29 May 2022).

Mason-Jones, A.J. and Loggie, J. (2020) 'Child sexual exploitation. An analysis of serious case reviews in England: poor communication, incorrect assumptions and adolescent neglect', *Journal of Public Health*, 42(1): 62–8.

Matthews, C., Eggers, S.M., Townsend, L, Aarø, L.E., de Vries, P.J., Mason-Jones, A.J., De Koker, P., McClinton Appollis, T., Mtshizana, Y., Koech, J., Wubs, A. and De Vries, H. (2016) 'Effects of PREPARE, a multi-component, school-based HIV and intimate partner violence (IPV) prevention programme on adolescent sexual risk behaviour and IPV: cluster randomised controlled trial', *AIDS and Behavior*, 20(9): 1821–40.

Matthews, S., Schiraldi, V. and Chester, L. (2018) 'Youth justice in Europe: experience of Germany, the Netherlands, and Croatia in providing developmentally appropriate responses to emerging adults in the criminal justice system', *Justice Evaluation Journal*, 1(1): 59–81.

McGuire, K. (2018) 'The embodiment of complex trauma in domestic minor sex trafficking victims and the dangers of misidentification', *Journal of Human Behavior in the Social Environment*, 29(4): 535–47.

McKibbin, G. and Humphreys, C. (2019) 'The perceptions of Australian workers about caring for sexually exploited children in residential care', *Child Abuse Review*, 28(6): 418–30.

McLeod, D.A., Jones, R. and Cramer, E.P. (2015) 'An evaluation of a school-based, peer-facilitated, healthy relationship program for at-risk adolescents', *Children & Schools*, 37(2): 108–16.

McNaughton Nicholls, C. Cockbain, C., Brayley, H., Harvey, S., Fox, S., Paskell, C., Ashby, M., Gibson, K. and Jago, N. (2014) *Research on the Sexual Exploitation of Boys and Young Men.* Ilford: Barnardo's.

McNeish, D. and Scott, S. (2018) *Key Messages from Research on Children and Young People Who Display Harmful Sexual Behaviour.* Essex: Centre of Expertise on Child Sexual Abuse.

Miller, E., Tancredi, D.J., McCauley, H.L., Decker, M.R., Virata, M.C.D., Anderson, H.A., O'Connor, B. and Silverman, J.G. (2013) 'One-year follow-up of a coach-delivered dating violence prevention program: a cluster randomized controlled trial', *American Journal of Preventive Medicine*, 45(1): 108–12.

Miller-Perrin, C. and Wurtele, S.K. (2017) 'Sex trafficking and the commercial sexual exploitation of children', *Women & Therapy*, 40(1–2): 123–51.

Muraya, D.N. and Fry, D. (2016) 'Aftercare services for child victims of sex trafficking: a systematic review of policy and practice', *Trauma, Violence, & Abuse*, 17(2): 204–20.

Murray, C.E., King, K. and Crowe, A. (2016) 'Understanding and addressing teen dating violence: implications for family counselors', *The Family Journal*, 24(1): 52–9.

National Youth Agency (2020) *Hidden in Plain Sight: Gangs and Exploitation.* Leicester: National Youth Agency.

NSPCC (National Society for the Prevention of Cruelty to Children) (2020) *How Safe Are Our Children? an Overview of Data on Abuse of Adolescents.* London: NSPCC.

Ofsted (Office for Standards in Education) (2011) *Ages of Concern: Learning Lessons from Serious Case Reviews.* Manchester: Ofsted.

Ofsted (2015) *Common Weaknesses in Local Authorities Judged Inadequate under the Single Inspection Framework: A Summary.* Manchester: Ofsted.

Ofsted (2019) *Safeguarding Children and Young People in Education from Knife Crime: Lessons from London.* Manchester: Ofsted.

Ofsted (2021) *Review of Sexual Abuse in Schools and Colleges.* Manchester: Ofsted.

Ofsted, CQC (Care Quality Commission), HMICFRS (HMI Constabulary and Fire & Rescue Services) and HMIP (HMI Probation) (2018) *Protecting Children from Criminal Exploitation, Human Trafficking and Modern Slavery: An Addendum.* Manchester: Ofsted.

Okech, D., Choi, Y.J., Elkins, J. and Burns, A.C. (2018) 'Seventeen years of human trafficking research in social work: a review of the literature', *Journal of Evidence-Informed Social Work*, 15(2): 103–22.

Ornellas, A., Spolander, G., Engelbrecht, L.K., Sicora, A., Pervova, I., Martínez-Román, M., Law, A.K., Shajahan, P.K., das Dores Guerreiro, M., Casanova, J.L., Garcia, M.L.T., Acar, H., Martin, L. and Strydomet, M. (2019) 'Mapping social work across 10 countries: structure, intervention, identity and challenges', *International Social Work*, 62(4): 1183–97.

Palmer, E. (2019) 'Trafficked children and child protection systems in the European Union', *European Journal of Social Work*, 22(4): 551–62.

Payne, M. (2020) *Modern Social Work Theory* (5th edn). London: MacMillan.

Pearce, J.J. (2014) '"What's going on" to safeguard children and young people from child sexual exploitation: a review of local safeguarding children boards' work to protect children from sexual exploitation', *Child Abuse Review*, 23(3): 159–70.

Perdue, T., Prior, M., Williamson, C. and Sherman, C. (2012) 'Social justice and spiritual healing: using micro and macro social work practice to reduce domestic minor sex trafficking', *Social Work & Christianity*, 39(4): 449–65.

Petering, R., Wenzel, S.L. and Winetrobe, H. (2014) 'Systematic review of current intimate partner violence prevention programs and applicability to homeless youth', *Journal of the Society for Social Work and Research*, 5(1): 107–35.

Pike, N., Langham, M. and Lloyd, S. (2019) *Parents' Experiences of the Children's Social Care System When a Child Is Sexually Exploited.* Leeds: Parents Against Child Exploitation.

Pona, I. and Turner, A. (2018) *Crumbling Futures: Why Vulnerable 16 and 17 Year Olds Need More Support as They Move into Adulthood.* London: The Children's Society.

Pritchard, D. and Svistak, M. (2014) *StreetChance: Understanding the Role StreetChance Can Play in Reducing Youth Crime and Anti-social Behaviour.* London: New Philanthropy Capital.

Public Health England (2020) *A Review of Interventions to Improve Mental Health and Wellbeing of Gang-Affiliated Young People: A Rapid Evidence Synthesis.* London: Public Health England.

Pullmann, M.D., Roberts, N., Parker, E.M., Mangiaracina, K. J., Briner, L., Silverman, M. and Becker, J.R. (2020) 'Residential instability, running away, and juvenile detention characterizes commercially sexually exploited youth involved in Washington State's child welfare system', *Child Abuse & Neglect*, 102: 104423.

Radford, L., Allnock, D. and Hynes, P. (2015) *Preventing and Responding to Child Sexual Abuse and Exploitation: Evidence Review.* New York: UNICEF.

Radford, L., Richardson Foster, H., Barter, C. and Stanley, N. (2017) *Rapid Evidence Assessment: What Can Be Learnt from Other Jurisdictions about Preventing and Responding to Child Sexual Abuse.* Preston: University of Central Lancashire.

Rap, S.E. (2015) 'The participation of social services in youth justice systems in Europe', *European Journal of Social Work*, 18(5): 675–89.

Reisel, A. (2017) 'Practitioners' perceptions and decision-making regarding child sexual exploitation – a qualitative vignette study', *Child & Family Social Work*, 22(3): 1292–301.

Ritchie, J., Spencer, L. and O'Connor, W. (2003) 'Carrying out qualitative analysis', in J. Ritchie and J. Lewis (eds) *Qualitative Research Practice.* London: Sage, pp 219–62.

Robinson, G., McLean, R. and Densley, J. (2019) 'Working County Lines: child criminal exploitation and illicit drug dealing in Glasgow and Merseyside', *International Journal of Offender Therapy and Comparative Criminology*, 63(5): 694–711.

Rogers, M., Rumley, T. and Lovatt, G. (2019) 'The Change Up project: using social norming theory with young people to address domestic abuse and promote healthy relationships', *Journal of Family Violence*, 34(6): 507–19.

Rogowski, S. (2010) 'Young offending: towards a radical/critical social policy', *Journal of Youth Studies*, 13(2): 197–211.

Sapiro, B., Johnson, L., Postmus, J.L. and Simmel, C. (2016) 'Supporting youth involved in domestic minor sex trafficking: divergent perspectives on youth agency', *Child Abuse & Neglect*, 58: 99–110.

Sawyer, S.M., Azzopardi, P.S., Wickremarathne, D. and Patton, G.C. (2018) 'The age of adolescence', *The Lancet Child and Adolescent Health*, 2: 223–8.

SCIE (Social Care Institute for Excellence) (2012) *Introduction to Children's Social Care*. London: Social Care Institute for Excellence.

Scotland's Commissioner for Children and Young People (2011) *Scotland: A Safe Place for Child Traffickers? A Study into the Nature and Extent of Child Trafficking in Scotland*. Edinburgh: Scotland's Commissioner for Children and Young People.

Scott, S., Botcherby, S. and Ludvigsen, A. (2017a) *Wigan and Rochdale Child Sexual Exploitation Innovation Project*. London: Department for Education.

Scott, S., Lloyd, S., Wright, C. and Ludvigsen, A. (2017b) *South Yorkshire Empower and Protect Child Sexual Exploitation Innovation Project: Evaluation Report*. London: Department for Education.

Scottish Government (2021) *National Guidance for Child Protection in Scotland 2021*. Edinburgh: The Scottish Government.

Shuker, L. (2015) 'Safe foster care for victims of child sexual exploitation', *Safer Communities*, 14(1): 37–46.

Shuker, L. (2018) *The Children and Social Work Act: The Role of Voluntary Sector CSE Services in New Safeguarding Arrangements*. Luton: University of Bedfordshire.

Sidebotham, P., Brandon, M., Bailey, S., Belderson, P., Dodsworth, J., Garstang, J., Harrison, E., Retzer, A. and Sorensen, P. (2016) *Pathways to Harm, Pathways to Protection: A Triennial Analysis of Serious Case Reviews 2011 to 2014*. London: Department for Education.

Spatscheck, C. and Wolf-Ostermann, K. (2009) *The Socio-spatial Paradigm in Social Work – Social Space Analyses as Method for Practitioners and Researchers,* Working Paper Series No. 1. Lund: Socialhögskolan, Lunds universitet.

Spratt, T., Nett, J., Bromfield, L., Hietamäki, J., Kindler, H. and Ponnert, L. (2014) 'Child protection in Europe: Development of an international cross-comparison model to inform national policies and practices', *British Journal of Social Work*, 45(5).

Stanley, T. and Guru, S. (2015) 'Childhood radicalisation risk: an emerging practice issue', *Practice*, 27(5): 353–66.

Stanley, Y. (2020) 'Dealing with risks to children outside the family home', Ofsted – Social Care and Early Years Regulation Blog. Available at: https://socialcareinspection.blog.gov.uk/2020/03/06/dealing-with-risks-to-children-outside-the-family-home/ (accessed 29 April 2022).

Stone, N. (2011) 'The "sexting" quagmire: criminal justice responses to adolescents' electronic transmission of indecent images in the UK and the USA', *Youth Justice*, 11(3): 266–81.

Stubbs, J. and Durcan, G. (2017) *Unlocking a Different Future: An Independent Evaluation of Project Future.* London: Centre for Mental Health.

Sturrock, R. (2012) *Supporting Transitions: A Summative Evaluation of the Transition to Adulthood Pilots.* London: Catch 22.

The Economist Intelligence Unit (2020) *Out of the Shadows: Shining Light on the Response to Child Sexual Abuse and Exploitation.* London: The Economist Intelligence Unit.

Thomas, R. and D'Arcy, K. (2017) 'Combatting child sexual exploitation with young people and parents: contributions to a twenty-first-century family support agenda', *British Journal of Social Work*, 47(6): 1686–703.

Turner, A., Belcher, L. and Pona, I. (2019) *Counting Lives Report: Responding to Children Who Are Criminally Exploited.* London: Children's Society.

Van de Vijver, K. and Harvey, R. (2019) 'Child sexual exploitation (CSE): applying a systemic understanding of "grooming" and the LUUUUTT model to aid second order change', *Journal of Family Therapy*, 41(3): 447–64.

Weale, S. (2020) 'Youth services suffer 70% funding cuts in less than a decade', *The Guardian*, 20 January. Available at: www.theguard ian.com/society/2020/jan/20/youth-services-suffer-70-funding-cut-in-less-than-a-decade (accessed 11 March 2022).

Welsh Government (2021) 'Safeguarding guidance'. Available at: https://gov.wales/safeguarding-guidance (accessed 11 March 2022).

Werkmeister Rozas, L., Ostrander, J. and Feely, M. (2018) 'Inequalities in US child protection: the case of sex trafficked youth', *Social Sciences*, 7(8): 135.

Wilkinson, J. (2018) *Developing and Leading Trauma-Informed Practice*, Devon: Research in Practice.

Williams, D.P. (2018) *Being Matrixed: The (Over)Policing of Gang Suspects in London*. London: StopWatch.

Williams, D.P. and Clarke, B. (2016) *Dangerous Associations: Joint Enterprise, Gangs and Racism*. London: Centre for Crime and Justice Studies.

Wroe, L.E. (2021) 'Young people and "County Lines": a contextual and social account', *Journal of Children's Services*, 16(1): 39–55.

Wroe, L.E. and Lloyd, J. (2020) 'Watching over or working with? Understanding social work innovation in response to extra-familial harm', *Social Sciences*, 9(4): 37.

Index

Note: References to figures appear in *italic* type;
those in **bold** type refer to tables.

R

racism 8, 53, 59, 83, 94
see also Black young people
radicalisation 5, 8, 12, 23, 27, 30,
    46, 65, 70, 101
reflective practice 20, 35, 38, 50,
    51, 55, 67, 89, 90, 101
Reisel, A. 51
relational safety 30, 35, 36, 40–2,
    86, 88–91, 97
relational violence, between young
    people *see* peers; peer-to-
    peer abuse
relationship-based social work 3,
    4, 6, 19, 24, 34–5, 66, 81,
    90–3, 109
  collaborative relationships 34,
    38–40
  community relationships 40–1
  and contextual approach 88–90,
    98, 109
  flexibility in 37, 38
  trusted relationships 34, 35–8
residential care 17–18, 79
responsibility
  of services 30, 77, 78, 92
  of young people for behaviour 9,
    10, 38, 82, 104
re-traumatisation 68, 85
Robinson, G. 71
Rogers, M. 56

S

Safe Choices Leaving Care and
    Custody Project Programme
    on Sexual Exploitation 36–7,
    82
Safe Dates (US) 54
safeguarding guidance
  England 5, 9, 11, 13, 14, 19, 23,
    47, 49, 60, 61, 106
  Northern Ireland 5
  Scotland 5, 10, 13, 23, 93
  Wales 5, 9–10, 13, 23, 49, 60, 61
safeguarding practice 1–3, 9–13
safety, of young people 20, 47, 54,
    55, 59, 61, 109
  and adolescent development 74

and collaborative relationships
    with parents/carers 39
relational approach 88–9,
    90, 109
right to 15
youth-centred approach 78, 79, 84
Sapiro, B. 80
Scandinavia 18
school-based interventions 41,
    54–5, 56–7
Scotland, child protection
    system 5, 10, 13, 23, 93
Scottish Children's Hearing
    System 10
Second Chance programme
    (US) 55–6
secure accommodation 15–16,
    17, 58
self-protection 76
serious youth violence 5, 8, 23,
    59, 70, 78, 89, 93
service redesign
  future, questions to guide **98–9**
  narrative of 91–2
sexism 53, 82
sexual abuse 30
  abuse through sexual image
    sharing 72
  harmful sexual behaviours 5, 41,
    60–1, 69, 79, 89
  peer-to-peer abuse 5, 12, 17, 23,
    36, 50, 60, 66, 89
  see also child sexual exploitation
    (CSE)
shortfalls, of safeguarding and
    welfare systems 6–7, 10
short-term interventions, need
    for 38, 77
Shuker, L. 49
social care 24, 47–8
  broadening the scope of 64–6
  and partnerships 52
social care responses 53–4,
    91–2, 94–5
  characteristics of effective and
    promising 26–7
  and community
    contexts 55–6, 58
  and human rights 107–8